C000232069

ISBN 978-0-266-87687-8
PIBN 10903161

This book is a reproduction of an important historical work. Forgotten Books uses
state-of-the-art technology to digitally reconstruct the work, preserving the original format
whilst repairing imperfections present in the aged copy. In rare cases, an imperfection in
the original, such as a blemish or missing page, may be replicated in our edition. We do,
however, repair the vast majority of imperfections successfully; any imperfections that
remain are intentionally left to preserve the state of such historical works.

FREE PUBLIC EXHIBITION

From Saturday, May 1, Until Time of Sale
Weekdays 9 a.m. to 6 p.m. · Sunday 2 to 5 p.m.

UNRESTRICTED PUBLIC SALE

Wednesday, Thursday and Friday
May 5, 6 and 7 at 2:15 p.m.

Exhibition and Sale at the

AMERICAN ART GALLERIES

MADISON AVENUE · 56th TO 57th STREET
New York City
1926

No. 597. Pair Magnificent French Wrought Iron Gates
(*By Jean Tijou, Made circa 1720*)

ENGLISH & FRENCH FURNITURE
OF THE AGES OF OAK · WALNUT & SATINWOOD
ORIENTAL AND EUROPEAN PORCELAINS
RENAISSANCE BRONZES AND A NUMBER
OF SUPERB XVI-XVII CENTURY TAPESTRIES

Sold By Order of

MR. H. F. DAWSON

Sales Conducted By Mr. O. Bernet & Mr. H. H. Parke

AMERICAN ART ASSOCIATION · INC.

Managers

CONDITIONS OF SALE

I. REJECTION OF BIDS: Any bid which is not commensurate with the value of the article offered, or which is merely a nominal or fractional advance, may be rejected by the auctioneer if in his judgment such bid would be likely to affect the sale injuriously.

II. THE BUYER: The highest bidder shall be the buyer, and if any dispute arises between two or more bidders, the auctioneer shall either decide the same or put up for re-sale the lot so in dispute.

III. IDENTIFICATION AND DEPOSIT BY BUYER: The name of the buyer of each lot shall be given immediately on the sale thereof, and when so required, each buyer shall sign a card giving the lot number, amount for which sold, and his or her name and address.

A deposit at the actual time of the sale shall be made of all or such part of the purchase prices as may be required.

If the two foregoing conditions are not complied with, the lot or lots so purchased may at the option of the auctioneer be put up again and re-sold.

IV. RISK AFTER PURCHASE: Title passes upon the fall of the auctioneer's hammer, and thereafter the property is at the purchaser's risk, and neither the consignor nor the Association is responsible for the loss of, or any damage to any article by theft, fire, breakage, however occasioned, or any other cause whatsoever.

V. DELIVERY OF PURCHASES: Delivery of any purchases will be made only upon payment of the total amount due for all purchases at the sale.

VI. RECEIPTED BILLS: Goods will only be delivered on presentation of a receipted bill. A receipted bill presented by any person will be recognized and honored as an order by the buyer, directing the delivery to the bearer of the goods described thereon. If a receipted bill is lost before delivery of the property has been taken, the buyer should immediately notify the Association of such loss.

VII. STORAGE IN DEFAULT OF PROMPT PAYMENT AND CALLING FOR GOODS: Articles not paid for in full and not called for by the purchaser or agent by noon of the day following that of the sale may be turned over by the Association to some carter to be carried to and stored in some warehouse until the time of the delivery therefrom to the purchaser, and the cost of such cartage and storage and any other charges will be charged against the purchaser and the risk of loss or damage occasioned by such removal or storage will be upon the purchaser.

In any instance where the purchase bill has not been paid in full by noon of the day following that of the sale, the Association and the auctioneer reserve the right, any other stipulation in these conditions of sale notwithstanding, in respect to any or all lots included in the purchase bill, at its or his option, either to cancel the sale thereof or to re-sell the same at public or private sale without further notice for the account of the buyer and to hold the buyer responsible for any deficiency and all losses and expenses sustained in so doing.

VIII. SHIPPING: Shipping, boxing or wrapping of purchases is a business in which the Association is in no wise engaged, but the Association will, however, afford to purchasers every facility for employing at current and reasonable rates carriers and packers; doing so, however, without any assumption of responsibility on its part for the acts and charges of the parties engaged for such service.

IX. GUARANTY: The Association exercises great care to catalogue every lot correctly and endeavors therein and also at the actual time of sale to point out any error, defect or imperfection, but guaranty is not made either by the owner or the Association of the correctness of the description, genuineness, authenticity or condition of any lot and no sale will be set aside on account of any incorrectness, error of cataloguing or imperfection not noted or pointed out. Every lot is sold "as is" and without recourse.

Every lot is on public exhibition one or more days prior to its sale, and the Association will give consideration to the opinion of any trustworthy expert to the effect that any lot has been incorrectly catalogued and in its judgment may thereafter sell the lot as catalogued or make mention of the opinion of such expert, who thereby will become responsible for such damage as might result were his opinion without foundation.

X. RECORDS: The records of the auctioneer and the Association are in all cases to be considered final and the highest bid shall in all cases be accepted by both buyer and seller as the value against which all claims for losses or damage shall lie.

XI. BUYING ON ORDER: Buying or bidding by the Association for responsible parties on orders transmitted to it by mail, telegraph, or telephone, if conditions permit, will be faithfully attended to without charge or commission. Any purchases so made will be subject to the foregoing conditions of sale, except that, in the event of a purchase of a lot of one or more books by or for a purchaser who has not through himself or his agent been present at the exhibition or sale, the Association will permit such lot to be returned within ten days from the date of sale, and the purchase money will be refunded, if the lot differs from its catalogue description.

Orders for execution by the Association should be given with such clearness as to leave no room for misunderstanding. Not only should the lot number be given, but also the title, and bids should be stated to be so much for the lot, and when the lot consists of one or more volumes of books or objects of art, the bid per volume or piece should also be stated. If the one transmitting the order is unknown to the Association, a deposit must be sent or reference submitted. Shipping directions should also be given.

PRICED CATALOGUES: Priced copies of the catalogue, or any session thereof, will be furnished by the Association at charges commensurate with the duties involved in copying the necessary information from the records of the Association.

These conditions of sale cannot be altered except by the auctioneer or by an officer of the Association.

AMERICAN ART ASSOCIATION, INC.
MANAGERS

OTTO BERNET
HIRAM H. PARKE
AUCTIONEERS

CATALOGUE

FOREWORD

IT is with pleasure that the unrestricted public sale is announced of the very distinctive collection of English furniture, tapestries. and objects of art assembled by the well-known antiquarian, Mr. H. F. Dawson of 9 East 56th Street. Mr. Dawson is removing from his present location, No. 9 East 56th Street, and pending the completion of his new establishment at No. 19 East 60th Street. has decided to dispose of his entire collection instead of storing it.

The collection now offered is replete with splendid specimens of English furniture from the ages of oak. walnut, mahogany and satinwood, many of them of most interesting provenance. A William and Mary walnut and marqueterie highboy, from the collections of Lord Francis Hope and Sir Arthur Cory-Wright, is a charming example of the delicate inlay of this period, when English marqueterie reached its highest standard of perfection. The Ranfurly suite of walnut furniture. carved in the Carolean style, during the Georgian period, and covered in the contemporary needlework. charged with the Ranfurly armorial bearings, is a unique specimen. The two mahogany armchairs from the Earl of Strathmore's collection, a set of twelve walnut and tooled leather armchairs from the collection of His Grace, the Duke of Northumberland, K. G., the three white mahogany armchairs, the design of which appears in Chippendale's original publication of *The Gentleman's and Cabinet-Maker's Director*, the carved mahogany tripod tea table, illustrated in *The Old World House* by Herbert Cescinsky, with an important 'master's chair', are examples of English eighteenth century furniture revealing the complete charm of the famous English cabinetmaker. Thomas Chippendale.

Of the few French objects, all of which are of great interest. attention must be given to the kingwood and tulipwood writing table by the *maître ébéniste* J. G. Schlichtig, of beautiful proportions and mounted with superbly modeled and chased ormolu. This master is represented in the Louvre by a commode bearing the monogram of Marie Antoinette.

The magnificent wrought iron gates by Jean Tijou, who achieved the incomparable gates at Hampton Court Palace, are undoubtedly the finest examples of wrought iron ever offered at auction.

The collection comprises a number of Renaissance tapestries, one extremely rare example of Delft weave by Karel van Mander, and a superbly woven 'pergola' tapestry. In addition, there are many fine specimens of Oriental and European porcelains, Renaissance bronzes, cushions in tapestry and needlework, brocades, velvets and old English crewel-work. A group of photograph frames covered in beautiful old brocades, damasks and velvets adds a distinctly original and very pleasing note to a highly valuable and interesting collection.

American Art Association, Inc.

FIRST SESSION

WEDNESDAY, MAY 5, AT 2:15 P. M.

Catalogue Numbers 1 to 219 Inclusive

~~~~

MISCELLANEOUS OBJECTS, BRONZES AND PORCELAINS

1. MOORISH MAJOLICA LUSTRED INKWELL

Rectangular, with serrated edges; the sides pierced with arcadings; in cobalt- and turquoise-blue and canary-yellow.

Height, 3½ inches.

2. NAILSEA GLASS PEN   *English, XVIII Century*

Interesting and rare specimen of glass made at the small village of Nailsea, near Bristol, England.

Length, 7 inches.

3. EIGHTEEN VENETIAN GLASSES   *Early, XIX Century*

Tumbler-shape; richly decorated in reds, blues, aubergine, green and old-gold, in varying designs.

4. LUSTRED FAIENCE VASE   *Persian, XVII Century*

Pear-shape; in cobalt-blue, displaying conventional foliage and animalistic figures. Fine metallic *reflets.*

Height, 4½ inches.

5. TWO FAMILLE-VERTE SWEETMEAT DISHES   *Ming*

Canary-yellow field, exhibiting domestic *chinoiserie* subjects.

Length, 5 inches.

6. PAIR PORCELAIN FLOWER-HOLDERS   *Chelsea, XVIII Century*

Tapering vase form, on circular base; with two leaf-scrolled handles. Finely glazed in turquoise-blue reserved in white with sprays of flowers. (Rim chipped.)

Height, 5½ inches.

7. IVORY-TONED PORCELAIN BOWL   *K'ang-hsi*

Tub-shaped, with ringed perifery; in fine ivory glaze and crackle; on three serpentined bracket feet.

Diameter, 6½ inches.

11

8. BRONZE INKSTAND   *Italian Renaissance*
Circular bowl, enriched with festooned drapery, supported by three
kneeling putti.

Height, 2¾ inches.

9. BRONZE STATUETTE   *Italian, XVIII Century*
Erect female figure with head inclined to the left, wearing loose
draperies. On rouge antique veined marble base.

Height of statuette, 5½ inches.

10. BRONZE INKSTAND   *Italian, XVI Century*
Triangular, with strap scrollings at the angles; acanthus cover with
terminal figure of a galeated Roman warrior. On leaf-molded feet.

Height, 6½ inches.

11. CELADON GILDED BRONZE INKSTAND   *K'ang-hsi*
Oriental female figure in celadon, seated before a flowering tree;
two branches fitted for candles. Ormolu mounts.

Height, 6 inches.

12. PAIR ITALIAN BRONZE CANDLESTICKS
Balustered stem, enriched with mascarons; on circular tray and
splayed base. Richly ornamented in the Renaissance manner.

Height, 8 inches.

13. THREE DECORATED PORCELAIN VASES
Swansea, XVIII Century
Ovoidal, with tapered neck, outcurving lip, and scrolled dolphin
handles; on circular foot and square plinth. The body depicting
old English rustic scenes in fine colors enriched with gilding.
(Slight restoration.)

Height of two, 8½ inches; the other, 9½ inches.

14. TWO DECORATED PORCELAIN VASES   *Chelsea, XVIII Century*
Triangular form, supported by three recumbent lions on incurving
base of the same contour; enriched with rams' masks at the upper
corners; in fine turquoise-blue; the panels reserved in white displaying bacchanalian scenes; gold anchor mark at base.

Height, 9¼ inches.

15. TWO DECORATED PORCELAIN BEAKER VASES   *Ch'ien-lung*
Cylindrical, with flaring lip and circular splayed base. Finely glazed
in mazarine-blue, the leaf-form panels reserved in white and depicting floral branches.

Height, 7 inches.

16. THREE IMPERIAL-YELLOW AND GREEN PORCELAIN DISHES

K'ang-hsi

37.50 Circular; the centre enriched with a circular medallion, enclosing scrollings in green and surrounded by cloud scrollings on an imperial-yellow ground. Six character marks at the back.

Diameter, 7¼ inches.

17. PAIR DECORATED PORCELAIN FLOWER-HOLDERS

Crown Derby, XVIII Century

150. Segmental; on incurving splayed base, with two classic strap handles. Decorated in characteristic colors, the reserved medallions portraying views of Naples and of the Vatican.

Height, 7½ inches.

18. GILDED GESSO COFFRET *Italian Renaissance*

22.50 Rectangular hinged top, with central Romayne portrait medallion, in a fine Renaissance motif; the sides with scrolled pilasters; on claw feet.

Length, 10 inches.

19. PAIR REPOUSSÉ PEWTER COVERED VASES

English, XVIII Century

100. Urn-shaped vase, with slightly domed cover having an acorn finial; and arched handles at the shoulders. Enriched with oval paterae and festoons of flowers enclosing two oval panels; on splayed circular foot. Inscribed at the base: URANIA, HUTTON, SHEFFIELD, 1805.

Height, 10 inches

20. PAIR BRONZE TAZZAS *French, Derectoire Period*

50. Calyx form, with scrolled branch handles; on Siena marble bases having bronze acanthus molding at the plinths.

Height, 11 inches; width, 8½ inches.

21. CRIMSON VELVET PHOTOGRAPH FRAME

30. Rectangular molded frame, covered in rich Renaissance velvet and banded with gold galloon; the interior and exterior with crimson damask.

Height, 12¾ inches; width, 11 inches.

22. CRIMSON VELVET PHOTOGRAPH FRAME

55. Rectangular molded frame, covered in rich Renaissance velvet and banded with gold galloon. Back in crimson damask.

Height, 12¾ inches; width, 11 inches.

13

23. INLAID BUHL INKSTAND *Louis Quatorze Period*
Rectangular, slightly *bombés* sides and front with concave tray for
pens; fitted with two compartments for inkwells; on four dolphin
supports.
Length, 12½ inches.

24. CRIMSON VELVET PHOTOGRAPH FRAME
Rectangular molded frame, covered in rich Renaissance velvet and
banded with gold galloon; the interior and exterior with crimson
damask.
Height, 12¾ inches; width, 11 inches.

25. CRIMSON DAMASK PHOTOGRAPH FRAME
Rectangular ogee-molded frame, covered in fine old crimson damask
and banded with silver galloon.
Height, 15¼ inches; width, 12¼ inches.

26. NEEDLEPOINT PHOTOGRAPH FRAME
Rectangular frame, covered in fine old English needlework and
crimson damask.
Height, 15¼ inches; width, 12 inches.

27. PAIR CLOISONNÉ ENAMEL COVERED VASES *K'ang-hsi*
Oviform, with short neck and domed cover. Decorated with floral
scrolls and leafage in polychrome, on a pure turquoise-blue ground.
Height, 15¼ inches.

28. SEMI-EGG-SHELL PORCELAIN VASE *Ch'ien-lung*
Oviform; brilliant gold ground patterned with small gaily colored
flowers and Chinese domestic scenes, reserved on creamy-white.
Height, 9½ inches.

29. PAIR DECORATED PORCELAIN VASES
Longton Hall, XVIII Century
Ovoid, with incurved neck, flaring broad lip and two mask handles.
Decorated in royal-blue, enriched with minute gold scrollings; three
panels reserved in white, exhibiting sprays of roses; the lip with
ivy in gold.
Height, 10 inches.

30. DECORATED PORCELAIN TWO-HANDLED URN
Worcester, XVIII Century
On rectangular plinth, the front displaying on a rose ground a
rustic scene; the urn enriched with budding leafage in high relief,
the handles of scrolled boughs. Enhanced by gilding.
Height, 10¼ inches.

14

31. DECORATED PORCELAIN CAKE BASKET
Royal Worcester, XVIII Century

60.— Oblong, with serrated edge; bail handle. Fine apple-green glaze enriched by gilding, depicting within a cartouche, reserved in white, Windsor Castle.

Length, 10½ inches.

32. DECORATED PORCELAIN COVERED BOWL *Ch'ien-lung*

60.— *Famille rose*, circular deep two-handled bowl with domed cover having a conical finial; richly decorated with *chinoiserie* motifs.

Diameter, 12½ inches.

33. PAIR DECORATED TWO-HANDLED COVERED URNS
Crown Derby, XVIII Century

150.— Glazed in deep rose, gilded and marbleized, portraying within panels naturalistic scenes of Dunraven Castle, Glenmorganshire and Fenthill Abbey, Wiltshire. The covers with pine finials.

Height, 12½ inches.

34. DECORATED VASE *Ch'ien-lung*

40.— Bottle form, with incurving neck and flaring lip. In finely glazed golden-yellow, enriched with branches of prunus blossoms in relief and a bird perched upon a bamboo branch.

Height, 11½ inches.

35. DECORATED BOWL ON TEAKWOOD STAND *Tao-kuang*

220.— Drum-shaped, with slightly tapering sides; richly decorated in emerald-green, *rouge de fer*, gold and blues, depicting exotic plants, birds, etc.

Height, 11½ inches; diameter, 21½ inches.

36. DECORATED PORCELAIN VASE *Crown Derby, XVIII Century*

70.— Classic urn-shape, with scrolled serpent handles in gold; the incurving neck enriched with palmate motifs, the perifery with rural English landscape scenes. Square base.

Height, 13½ inches.

37. FAMILLE-ROSE JAR *Ch'ien-lung*

00.— Oviform, with high shoulder and wide short neck. White ground decorated with brilliantly colored floral sprays and a full plumaged bird. On carved teakwood stand.

Height, 13¼ inches.

38. DECORATED PORCELAIN VASE *Ch'ien-lung*

120.— Ovoid, with incurving neck and flaring lip; on domed foot. Enriched in the fine characteristic *famille verte* and *famille rose*, depicting within a scrolled cartouche a landscape and river scene.

Height, 14 inches.

15

39. ELEVEN ASSORTED PIECES OF PORCELAIN
Lowestoft, XVIII Century

Comprising: Four octagonal deep plates; one plate; two dishes; two creamers; and two small deep dishes, decorated in the oriental manner in blue and rose-color.

40. PORCELAIN DESSERT SERVICE   *Worcester, XVIII Century*

Comprising: Two dessert plates, four square, three oval and two shell-shaped fruit dishes. Decorated in fine reds, blues and greens with foliage and fruit. (Two restored.)

41. BLUE AND WHITE PORCELAIN DINNER SERVICE   *Spode*

Comprising: Seven dinner plates, six soup plates, six graduated platters, four assorted covered vegetable dishes, two uncovered vegetable dishes and two gravy boats. Decorated on a white ground in fine blue, portraying old English rustic scenes.

42. URBINO MAJOLICA JAR

Oviform; enriched with a circular medallion exhibiting a profile bust portrait of a regal male figure; facing right. In the characteristic colors of Urbino. (Restored.)
Height, 13½ inches.

43. FAMILLE-ROSE PLAQUE   *Ch'ien-lung*

Circular, with deep cavetto depicting a bird perched upon rockery with chysanthemums; the marli enriched with floral sprays. Finely glazed in rose, powder-blue and *rouge de fer*.
Diameter, 13½ inches.

44. PAIR DECORATED PORCELAIN COVERED VASES
Coalbrook Dale, XVIII Century

Pear-shape, on splayed circular foot, domed cover with cone finial. Beautiful turquoise-blue, the reserved medallions depicting nymphs with amorini, and naturalistic flowers. The whole enriched by gilding. (One cover with slight crack.)
Height, 14½ inches.

45. FAMILLE VERTE PLAQUE   *K'ang-hsi*

Deep plate with central medallion, exhibiting in characteristic colors a floral motif, the serrated edges a strapwork of cartouches enclosing differing motifs.
Diameter, 15½ inches.

16

46. PAIR GILDED BRONZE CANDLELABRA   *English, XVIII Century*
20. —Finely modeled infant satyr by the stump of a tree, supporting two grapevine branches, fitted for lights. Circular base.

Height, 14½ inches.

From the Collection of Lady Arthur Paget, Belgrave Square, London.

47. TWO BRONZE STATUETTES   *French, XVIII Century*
70. — MOLIÈRE AND RACINE. Finely modeled erect figures. On Siena marble bases with bronze plinths.

Height of statuettes, 14½ inches; of base, 11½ inches

48. TWO METAL AND GILDED BRONZE URNS
French, Directoire Period
20. —Classic form, with domed cover, cone finial, and two upright loop handles. The body enriched with finely chased ormolu mountings of palmate and leaf motifs; on rouge antique marble base; ball feet.

Height, 17¾ inches.

49. PAIR BRONZE CANDELABRA   *English, Empire Period*
Semi-draped negro child with gilded loincloth, supporting two
--0. —branches for lights. Circular base, claw feet.   *Height, 19 inches.*

From the Collection of Lady Arthur Paget, Belgrave Square, London.

50. BLUE AND WHITE PORCELAIN VASE   *K'ang-hsi*
Beaker-shaped, with tall neck and expanding lip; on splayed circular
5. base, enriched with scrollings and blooms of peonies; in fine cobalt-blue; paneled at the shoulder, base and lip. (Slight imperfections.)

Height, 21 inches.

51. BLUE AND WHITE VASE   *K'ang-hsi*
Inverted pear-shape, with short neck and outcurving lip. The body
40, — enriched with a succession of panels depicting small flowering trees. On gilded bronze square base.   *Height, 23 inches.*

52. PAIR WEDGWOOD GILDED BRONZE CANDELABRA
English, XVIII Century
40. —Slender shaft, with two adjustable scrolled arms and *bobêches* for lights and supports for shades; on circular jasper base and foot.

Height, 22 inches.

53. DECORATED PORCELAIN TABLE LAMP   *Ch'ien-lung*
Oviform, with incurving neck and domed foot; richly decorated on
0. —a glazed white ground with two rustic maidens and a stork; on gilded bronze base. Old-gold silk shade trimmed with fringe.

Height, 29 inches.

54. PAIR GILDED BRONZE CANDELABRA   *English, Directoire Period*
Tall fluted column, supported by three chimeric figures adorsed: surmounted by an urn emitting five branches for lights.   Stork finials.

Height, 27 inches.

From the Collection of Lady Arthur Paget, Belgrave Square, London.

55. AMERICAN GLAZED POTTERY TABLE LAMP
Sang-de-boeuf oviform vase, mounted on a *cuivre doré* base, adapted as a lamp, with fawn cut velvet domed shade, deep fringe and Chinese gilt figure finial.

Height, 49 inches.

TEXTILES

56. EMBROIDERED BLUE SATIN PURSE   *English, circa* 1709
Worked by E. Webb, wife of General Webb, an officer of the Duke of Marlborough's army at the Battle of Malplaquet.

57. EMBROIDERED SILK PURSE   *Stuart Period*
Lunette-shape, finely embroidered in gold and silver threads, exhibiting conventional floral motif.

58. NEEDLEPOINT SMALL TEA COZY   *English, XVIII Century*
Lunette-shape, exhibiting in fine tent-stitch and *petit point* a landscape scene, with a stag and a rabbit in the foreground.   Fine color.

59. THREE DRAP D'OR CUT VELVET CUSHIONS
Italian, XVIII Century
Square; in fine crimson cut velvet, exhibiting a bold floral design on an old-gold ground.   Trimmed with ball tassels at each corner.

60. GOLD-EMBROIDERED ROSE-CRIMSON BROCATELLE CUSHION
Italian Renaissance
Oblong; the central panel depicting within a canopied niche a saintly figure.   Crimson damask back.   Trimmed with short fringe.

61. GOLD-EMBROIDERED CRIMSON VELVET CUSHION
Italian Renaissance
Square; the central panel gold-embroidered, depicting within an oval medallion a saintly figure enclosed by gold galloon.   The back in fine floral crimson damask.

62. AMETHYST VELVET PHOTOGRAPH FRAME

Rectangular molded frame, covered in fine old velvet and banded with silver galloon. Back in golden-yellow damask.

Height, 15½ inches; width, 12 inches.

63. CRIMSON VELVET PHOTOGRAPH FRAME

Rectangular molded frame, covered in rich Renaissance velvet and banded with gold galloon; the interior and exterior with crimson damask.

Height, 15 inches; width, 12 inches.

64. SILK BROCADE PHOTOGRAPH FRAME

Rectangular frame, covered in fine old French floral brocade and banded with gold galloon.

Height, 15 inches; width, 12 inches.

65. SILK BROCADE PHOTOGRAPH FRAME

Rectangular frame, covered in fine old rose-crimson floral brocade.

Height, 15 inches; width, 12 inches.

66. GREEN DAMASK CUSHION   *English, XVIII Century*

Oblong; displaying a diaper patterning enclosing conventional leafage. Trimmed with narrow fringe.

67. AMETHYST VELVET AND BROCATELLE CUSHION

Approximately square; banded with cut velvet galloon, enclosing a panel of brocatelle. Trimmed with varicolored fringe.

68. GREEN CUT VELVET PHOTOGRAPH FRAME

Rectangular molded frame, covered in fine Renaissance cut velvet banded with silver galloon.

Height, 15 inches; width, 12 inches.

69. GREEN CUT VELVET PHOTOGRAPH FRAME

Similar to the preceding.

Height, 15 inches; width, 12 inches.

70. SILK BROCADE PHOTOGRAPH FRAME

Rectangular frame, covered in fine old French floral brocade and banded with silver galloon.

Height, 15 inches; width, 12 inches.

71. SILK BROCADE PHOTOGRAPH FRAME

Similar to the preceding.

Height, 15 inches; width, 12 inches.

19

72. SILK DAMASK PHOTOGRAPH FRAME

Rectangular frame, covered in fine old blue damask and banded with green silk galloon. The back in golden-yellow damask.

Height, 15¼ inches; width, 12 inches.

73. BLUE DAMASK STATIONERY HOLDER

Rectangular compartmented tray, with ogival arched back; covered in peacock-blue Spitalfields silk damask.

Height, 7 inches; length, 13 inches.

74. NEEDLEPOINT PHOTOGRAPH FRAME

Rectangular frame, covered in fine old English needlework and peacock-blue Spitalfields silk damask.

Height, 15 inches; width, 11½ inches.

75. BROCADED SILK BOUDOIR BASKET

Rectangular, with ogival arched top, covered in fine ivory silk brocade enriched with a floral motif in silk and silver threads; edged with silver galloon.

Height, 17½ inches.

76. NEEDLEPOINT PHOTOGRAPH FRAME

Rectangular frame, covered in fine old English needlework and moss-green Spitalfields silk damask.

Height, 15 inches; width, 12½ inches.

77. CRIMSON VELVET PHOTOGRAPH FRAME

Rectangular molded frame, covered in rich Renaissance velvet and banded with gold galloon; the interior and exterior with crimson damask.

Height, 15 inches; width, 12 inches.

78. CRIMSON SILK AND GOLD APPLIQUÉ EMBROIDERED CUSHION
Italian Renaissance

Oblong: the central panel superbly wrought in golden needlepoint, depicting a Virgin Martyr before a mountainous landscape. The back in rose-crimson silk. Trimmed with gold tassels at the corners.

79. FOUR OLD ENGLISH EMBROIDERED STOMACHERS

(A and B) Blue silk and old-rose silk; Georgian Period.
(C and D) Ivory silk and satin; William and Mary Period.

80. CRIMSON VELVET AND BROCATELLE DALMATIC
Italian Renaissance

Fluctuating tones. of fine velvet with inset panels of brocatelle *semé* with a small palmette motif. Banded in gold galloon.

81. CRIMSON VELVET AND BROCATELLE DALMATIC
Italian Renaissance
Similar to the preceding.

82. GREENISH-BLUE VELVET COVERLET   *Italian Renaissance*
Fluctuating tones. with the impress of previous appliqué embroid-ery. Bordered with *drap d'or* cut velvet galloon. Trimmed with blue and gold tasseled fringe.

46 by 22 inches.

83. LACE TABLE COVERLET   *Spanish, XVII Century*
In drawn-work, exhibiting fifteen circular medallions of differing design. Deep fringe.

Length, 61 inches; width, 37 inches.

84. JADE-GREEN VELVET COVERLET   *Italian, XVII Century*
Of beautiful deep tone: banded with silver galloon.

Length, 28½ inches; width, 23 inches.

85. THREE RUBY-RED VELVET PANELS   *Italian Renaissance*
Fluctuating tones. banded with silver galloon.

Length, 41 inches; width, 23 inches.

86. THREE RUBY-RED VELVET PANELS   *Italian Renaissance*
Similar to the preceding. differing in size.

Length, 20 inches; width, 17½ inches.

87. GOLD-EMBROIDERED SILK APPLIQUÉ CHASUBLE
Spanish Renaissance
Ivory moiré silk field: the back portraying within the Latin cross a needlepainted depiction of the Madonna and Child flanked by a seraph and a cherub: the holy Mother robed in finely shaded crimson and blue: around are scrollings in gold appliqué and roses. embroidered in silken threads.

88. EMBROIDERED SILK DALMATIC   *Italian Renaissance*
Ivory moiré silk ground. richly embroidered in gold and silken threads. displaying a central fan-shape motif. surrounded by scrolled leafage in gold and foliations in blues. roses. greens and peach tones; delicately blended.

89. CUT VELVET PANEL   *Italian Renaissance*
Rich central panel of cut velvet displaying on an ivory ground a floral motif in green, peach tones, and reds. flanked by panels of crimson cut velvet. Front of a chasuble.

21

90. CUT VELVET PANEL   *Italian Renaissance*
Similar to the preceding. Portion of a chasuble.

91. ROSE-CRIMSON SILK BROCADE COVERLET
                French, XVIII Century
Deep rich field exhibiting floral sprays. Old-gold fringe.
Length, 37 inches; width, 20 inches.

92. APPLIQUÉ EMBROIDERED SILK AND DAMASK COVERLET
                Italian, XVII Century
Central panel of *vieux rose* silk, appliqué with fine Renaissance design, flanked by golden-yellow damask: banded with gold galloon and fringe.   *Length, 48 inches; width, 22 inches.*

93. SILK BROCADE COVERLET   *French, XVIII Century*
Bleu-de-ciel field *semé* with scrollings, floral blossoms, banded by gold galloon.
Length, 36 inches; width, 21½ inches.

94. NEEDLEPOINT STRIP   *English, XVIII Century*
The field of *point d'Hongrie*, exhibiting a floral design in *petit point* in écru, blues, reds and greens.
Length, 5 feet 11 inches; width, 10½ inches

95. BRILLIANT BLUE SILK BROCADE COVER
                French, XVIII Century
Bleu-de-ciel field *semé* with floral sprays within ogival arches.
Length, 6 feet 9 inches; width, 4 feet 8 inches.

96. PEACH-TONED SILK BROCADE COVER   *French, XVIII Century*
Fluctuating field, displaying an allover patterning of conventional foliations in shaded yellow-green and blue.
Length, 6 feet 9 inches; width, 5 feet 8 inches.

97. PEACH-TONED SILK BROCADE PANEL   *French, XVIII Century*
Fluctuating tones exhibiting an allover floral motif in blue-green, ivory and gold.
Length, 9 feet 7 inches; width, 1 foot 7 inches.

98. BRUSSELS TAPESTRY CANTONNIÈRE   *Flemish, XVIII Century*
Finely woven in browns, fawns, blues, green and dull reds, depicting scrolled leafage and floral motifs, framed in a strapwork of circular medallions.
Height, 9 feet 6 inches; length, 6 feet 9 inches; depth at top, 1 foot 2 inches
width at sides, 1 foot 1 inch.

FURNITURE

99. MAHOGANY AND SHEFFIELD PLATE TEA TRAY

English, XVIII Century

Irregular octagonal mahogany tray, with arcaded Sheffield plate gallery; on embryonic claw feet.

Length, 29½ inches.

100. EMPIRE ORMOLU MANTEL CLOCK *By Bergmiller, à Paris*

Circular white enameled dial; urn-shaped case, supported by scrolled volutes terminating in claw feet; at the shoulders are winged grotesques flanking a displayed eagle.

Height, 15½ inches; width, 8½ inches.

101. CARVED MAHOGANY WALL BRACKET *English, XVIII Century*

Outset rectangular top, with leaf and dentil moldings from which are suspended chains of pendant husks; on three rosetted incurving laureled supports.

Height, 16½ inches; width, 14 inches.

102. OLD ENGLISH MAHOGANY CANTERBURY

Rectangular; the body fitted with shallow drawer; above are arcadings of spindles forming compartments for music and papers.

Height, 21½ inches; width, 19½ inches.

103. GEORGIAN BRASS FENDER

Front and rounded ends pierced with arcadings; on embryonic claw feet.

Length, 37 inches.

104. GEORGIAN BRASS FENDER

Pierced to a conventional design, with a central horizontal torus molding. On five pad feet.

Height, 10 inches; length, 40 inches.

105. PAIR WALNUT CANDLESTANDS *Queen Anne Period*

Twisted spiraled shaft, with circular dish top; on splayed circular base.

Height, 33½ inches; diameter, 7 inches.

106. TWO ADAM CARVED AND GILDED WALL SCONCES

English, XVIII Century

Graceful caryatid figure, with arms outstretched supporting two branches each emitting three scrolled boughs in *papier maché*, fitted with *bobèches* for lights.

Height, 32 inches; extension, 12 inches.

107. MAHOGANY BRACKET CLOCK   *English, XVIII Century*
Rectangular domed case, and bail handle; on bracket feet. Circular chased dial and richly engraved interior movement.
Height, 20 inches; width, 10½ inches.

108. LADY'S SHERATON INLAID SATINWOOD WRITING-DESK
English, XVIII Century
Rectangular galleried top with slant-front; recessed beneath and fitted at the side with a box drawer and two small drawers. On slender baluster legs with shelf stretcher.
Height, 36 inches; width, 16½ inches.

109. CARVED AND GILDED WALL MIRROR   *English, XVIII Century*
Arched oblong mirror; the frame leaf-molded, enclosing a scratch-carved quatrefoil motif; arched cresting composed of reversed C-scrolls and leafage; from the shoulders are suspended branches of oak leaves.   *Height, 47½ inches; width, 31 inches.*

110. CUT CRYSTAL CANDELABRUM   *English, XVIII Century*
Knopped and lanceolate stem, with pagoda top and urn finial, from which depend graceful chains of pendent drops, emitting four branches, two having *bobèches* for candles; on bronze gilded base enriched with panels of blue jasper Wedgwood ware.
Height, 26¼ inches.

111. PAIR BRONZE AND CUIVRE DORÉ CANDELABRA
Louis Seize Period
Erect winged putto, supporting a cornucopia emitting four branches with urn-shaped *bobèches* for candles. On circular *rouge antique* marble base having an echinus molding. Finely modeled figure.
Height, 30 inches.

112. PAIR CARVED AND GILDED TRIPOD PEDESTALS
English Directoire Period
Circular onyx marble top, banded by ormolu; the frieze enriched with oval paterae, connected by encarpa motifs. On tripod support; claw feet and incurving plinth. (One damaged.)
Height, 33½ inches.

113. EMBROIDERED SATIN MAHOGANY POLE SCREEN
English, XVIII Century
Heart-shape frame, enclosing embroidered satin panel, depicting in central medallion a child surrounded by ivy leafage. On graceful tripod support.
Height, 58½ inches; width, 17 inches.

24

114. EMBROIDERED SATIN MAHOGANY POLE SCREEN
English, XVIII Century
Similar to the preceding: with slight variation in embroidered design.
Height, 58½ inches; width, 17 inches.

115. OAK JOINT STOOL
Jacobean Period
Rectangular molded top and underframing; on columnar-turned legs with block feet and knees, connected by box stretcher.
Height, 18½ inches; width, 17½ inches.

116. WALNUT SIDE TABLE
Spanish, XVIII Century
Oblong massive top; the box frieze fitted with two end-on paneled drawers with knop handles. On turned and block stretchered legs.
Height, 28 inches; length, 36 inches.

117. WALNUT SIDE TABLE
Spanish, XVIII Century
Similar to the preceding, with slight variation in knop handles.
Height, 28 inches; length, 34½ inches.

118. ELM WINDSOR ARMCHAIR
English, XVIII Century
Comb-back. with seven spindles, molded arms and turned supports; panel seat; on turned H-stretchered legs.

119. PAINTED AND GILDED ARMCHAIR
English, Directoire Period
Oblong back and seat. covered in eighteenth century Venetian blue brocade; on curule legs, the framework enriched with an astragal molding and leafage.

120. TWO ELM WINDSOR ARMCHAIRS
English, XVIII Century
Comb-back. with pierced vase-shaped splat, flanked by four spindles: molded arms on balustered uprights: saddle seat, on turned outspreading stretchered legs.

121. SHERATON INLAID MAHOGANY JARDINIÈRE VELVET FIRE SCREEN
English, XVIII Century
Oblong arched frame, enriched with satinwood and hollywood inlay, exhibiting oval paterae and festoons of pendent husks enclosing an oval panel of cut jardinière velvet in crimson and green. On splayed end supports.
Height, 46½ inches; width, 25 inches.

122. SHERATON MAHOGANY NEST OF FOUR TABLES
English, XVIII Century
Oblong top. with rounded corners: balustered stretchered supports and splayed feet.
Height, 30 inches: width, 20 inches.

123. TWO SATINWOOD THREE-TIERED SIDE TABLES
English, XVIII Century

Panel back; three segmental tiers, the top galleried; on turned tapering legs.

Height, 36 inches; width, 18 inches.

124. TWO CARVED WALNUT FAUTEUILS   Régence Period

Cartouche-shaped back and seat, cannés; open splayed arms; on slightly cabriole legs terminating in leaf feet. Loose seat cushion and valance in eighteenth century silk floral brocade.

125. GEORGIAN GILDED WALL MIRROR
English, XVIII Century

Oblong mirror, above which is a jade-green and silvered glass panel depicting foliations enclosed within reeded half columns, surmounted by Corinthian capitals; the concave frieze with ball pendants.

Height, 58 inches; width, 32½ inches.

126. SHERATON MAHOGANY NEST OF FOUR TABLES
English, XVIII Century

Quadrangular serpentined top; on very delicate baluster legs, unusual supports. Very finely grained mahogany.

Height, 30 inches; width, 21½ inches.

127. SHERATON SATINWOOD SIDE CHAIR   English, XVIII Century

Open square cannés back and seat; on round tapering legs.

128. TWO ELM WINDSOR ARMCHAIRS   English, XVIII Century

Comb-back, with pierced vase-shaped splat flanked by three spindles; balustered uprights and molded arms; saddle-seat, on turned outspreading legs connected by incurving stretcher.

129. SHERATON MAHOGANY FOLDING SIDE TABLE
English, circa 1790

Rectangular molded folding top, which turns on a pivot, and reveals deep receptacle; paneled by a fine echinus molding. Supported by an interestingly reversed scrolled curule-shaped reeded support, with brass-bound toes.

Height, 29 inches; extended, 36 inches square.

130. SHERATON MAHOGANY FOLDING SIDE TABLE
English, circa 1790

Similar to the preceding.

Height, 29 inches; extended, 36 inches square.

131. SET OF SIX WALNUT SIDE CHAIRS   *Italian Renaissance*
O.—Oblong serpentined back and approximately square seat, covered in original brown leather; supported on trumpet-turned and block stretchered legs with bun feet.

(*Illustrated*)

132. SET OF SIX WALNUT SIDE CHAIRS   *Italian Renaissance*
O.—Similar to the preceding. One seat uncovered.

133. SHERATON NEST OF FOUR INLAID SATINWOOD TABLES
English, XVIII Century
O.—Rectangular top, paneled with applied moldings of ebony, enclosing oval medallions of amboyna wood; on ringed spindle supports; splayed feet.
Height, 27 inches; width, 19½ inches.

134. INLAID WALNUT LOWBOY   *English, Early XVIII Century*
O—Rectangular molded top; the front fitted with one long drawer and three small drawers, having reticulated brasses with bail handles; cyma-curved valance: on cabriole legs terminating in pad feet.
Height, 28 inches; length, 29½ inches.

27

135. HEPPLEWHITE MAHOGANY WINDOW SEAT
English, XVIII Century
Serpentined seat and arm-rests covered in old-rose floriated bro-
cade with tassels; on turned tapering legs.
Height, 28½ inches; length, 36½ inches.

136. WALNUT SIDE TABLE
Spanish, XVII Century
Rectangular overhanging top; the frieze fitted with one drawer flat-
carved to a lozenge motif, flanked by quatrefoils. On reel- and
knop-turned box stretchered legs; bun feet.
Height, 28½ inches; lenth, 29 inches.

137. SHERATON INLAID SATINWOOD SIDE TABLE
English, XVIII Century
Serpentined oblong top with arched ends banded with acajou; the
underframing of the same contour having lines of pencil-inlay; on
square tapering legs. *Height, 28½ inches; width, 38½ inches.*

138. TWO CARVED WALNUT SGABELLO CHAIRS *Italian Renaissance*
Oblong seat, with flat-carved circular medallion and incurving corners; on lyre-shape supports, the front carved with foliage and
embryonic claw-and-ball feet. The back, of similar contour, en-
closes scrolled escutcheon.

139. CARVED AND GILDED OVAL MIRROR *English, XVIII Century*
Oval molded frame, surmounted by a displayed eagle perched upon
a rocaille structure, flanked by scrolled leafage.
Height, 50 inches; width, 26½ inches.

140. INLAID WALNUT DRESSING TABLE *Queen Anne Period*
Oblong molded top with a line of sycamore inlay, rounded front
corners; front with one long drawer and two small drawers trimmed
with chased bat's-wing brasses; on cabriole legs terminating in pad
feet. Valanced apron. *Height, 29 inches; length, 29½ inches.*

141. TWO CARVED WALNUT SIDE CHAIRS *Italian Renaissance*
Rectangular back, enriched with acanthus leaf finials, which, with
the seat, is covered in fine crimson and gold brocatelle finished with
deep fringe; on spirally twisted H-stretchered legs having turned
pointed toes.

142. TWO CARVED WALNUT SIDE CHAIRS *Italian Renaissance*
Similar to the preceding.

143. INLAID SATINWOOD PEMBROKE TABLE *English, XVIII Century*
Oblong top, with two serpentined drop-leaves banded in acajou; the frieze with one drawer; on quadrangular tapering legs, with spade feet.

Height, 27 inches; length extended, 39½ inches

144. SMALL SHERATON AMBOYNA WOOD SOFA TABLE
English, XVIII Century
—Oblong top enriched with mahogany inlay, having two rule-jointed leaves with rounded corners; the frieze fitted with drawer trimmed with knop handles; on octagonal twin-column end supports braced by knopped central traverse. Splayed feet.

Height, 29 inches; length extended, 33½ inches

145. OAK GATE-LEG TABLE *English, XVII Century*
Oval top, with two rule-jointed flaps; frieze drawer; knopped turned legs, stretcher and two gates.

Height, 28 inches; length extended, 38½ inches.

146. CARVED MAHOGANY AND PARCEL-GILDED OVER-MANTEL MIRROR
English, XVIII Century
—Oblong mirror, enclosed within three panels of painted glass, the horizontal panel depicting a scene from the battle of the Lapithae and Centaurs; the leaf-carved frieze surmounted by a surbased arch enclosing classic mask.

Height, 57 inches; width, 48½ inches.

147. SET OF SIX MAHOGANY SIDE CHAIRS *Chippendale Period*
Open square back, with scrolled crowning rail and four vertical bar slats; "stretched up" square seats; on quadrangular stretchered legs. Three covered in leather, three in striped green-and-gold haircloth.

148. CARVED MAHOGANY OCTAGONAL TABLE
English, XVIII Century
—Octagonal tilting top, with leaf-carved edges; on vase baluster and tripod support, carved with chains of pendent fuchsia drops.

Height, 27 inches; diameter, 31 inches.

149. CARVED MAHOGANY OCTAGONAL TABLE
English, XVIII Century
—Oblong top, with two rule-jointed leaves, the edges carved with bandings and quatrefoils; small frieze drawer with loop drop handles. On reeded round legs.

Height, 28½ inches; length extended, 38½ inches.

29

150. OAK CRICKET TABLE *Queen Anne Period*

— Circular, with triangular box frieze; supported by three molded polygonal stretchered legs.

Height, 26 inches; diameter, 29½ inches.

151. SHERATON MAHOGANY DROP-LEAF TABLE
English, Late XVIII Century

Square molded top, with two drop-leaves; fitted with frieze drawer; on turned shaft with arched support and four brass claw feet.

Height, 28½ inches; length, 39 inches.

152. CARVED AND GILDED OVAL WALL MIRROR
English, XVIII Century

Oval mirror; the frame richly carved with rocaille-rococo motifs; the arched cresting centring within C-scrollings a shell.

Height, 69 inches; width, 33½ inches.

153. HEPPLEWHITE MAHOGANY OVAL BREAKFAST TABLE
English, XVIII Century

Extension table with one leaf; box frieze; supported by eight quadrangular legs.

Height, 29 inches; diameter, 47 inches.

154. PAIR PAINTED AND PARCEL-GILDED MAHOGANY HANGING BOOKCASES *English, XVIII Century*

Adam design; four graduated shelves, crested by an arched pediment enriched by a classic urn emitting a honeysuckle motif, flanked by swags of pendent husks; the base with two drawers enhanced by vases and festoons of drapery.

Height, 5 feet 5 inches; width, 2 feet 10 inches

155. PAIR SHERATON INLAID MAHOGANY CARD TABLES
English, XVIII Century

Serpentined oblong folding top, enriched with central medallion depicting sporting putti, surmounted by a classic mask emitting festoons of pendent husks; the shaped valance similarly enriched by satinwood inlay. On tapering cabriole legs.

Height, 28 inches; length, 36 inches.

156. VENETIAN BROCADE WALNUT WING CHAIR
Queen Anne Period

Serpentined oblong back and wings, outscrolling arms covered in beautiful peach-toned brocade with a floral motif finely wrought in gold and silken threads. On bracketed cabriole legs with pointed pad feet and leaf-carved knees.

30

157. OAK SLEIGH SEAT   *Flemish Renaissance*

Serpentined back and closed arms; on molded supports carved with
quatrefoils. Covered in contemporary moss-green damask; enriched
by a panel of embroidered velvet, displaying a medallioned saintly
figure and arabesqued scrollings.

158. TWO PAINTED CARVED AND GILDED PEDESTALS

English, XVIII Century

Rectangular canalated tapering columns, on molded leaf-carved
plinth; the oblong capital enriched with an urn-shape vase with satyr
masks and festoons of flowers and having an incurving superstructure.

Height, 52 inches.

159. MAHOGANY TRIPOD TABLE   *English, XVIII Century*

Circular top; on vase baluster and tripod support.

Height, 27½ inches; diameter, 30½ inches.

160. OAK GATE-LEG TABLE   *Jacobean Period*

Oblong top, with two folding flaps; the underframing containing
one small drawer. On vase baluster legs and gates.

Height, 26 inches; length extended, 36½ inches.

161. ADAM STEEL FIRE GRATE WITH IRON FONDÉ BACK

English, XVIII Century

The back depicting a shepherdess; the front serpentined and latticed, alternating with oval patera. Enriched with classic urn
finials.

Height, 40 inches; width, 30½ inches.

162. INLAID WALNUT DRESSING TABLE   *Queen Anne Period*

Oblong molded top, cleft at the corners; the front fitted with one
long frieze drawer and two small drawers, flanking the central
ogival arch. Slightly cabriole legs with pad feet.

Height, 29½ inches; length, 32 inches.

163. INLAID WALNUT KNEEHOLE WRITING-DESK

English, XVIII Century

Rectangular molded top; the front fitted with long frieze drawer,
valanced kneehole drawer and central recessed cupboard door
flanked by three smaller drawers. Trimmed with pierced bat's-wing
brasses and bail handles; bracket feet.

Height, 28½ inches; length, 34 inches.

31

164. OAK GATE-LEG TABLE   *Jacobean Period*

Oval top, with two folding flaps; supported by simply turned baluster legs and gates.   *Height, 29½ inches; length extended, 56 inches.*

165. MAHOGANY SOFA TABLE   *English, XVIII Century*

Oblong top, with two drop-leaves having rounded corners; the
frieze fitted with two end-on cock-beaded drawers and knop handles;
on quadrangular end supports with reeded curule feet and brass
toes, braced by central turned stretcher.
      Height, 27 inches; length, 57 inches.

166. WROUGHT IRON TORCHÈRE   *Scotch Gothic*

Slender stem, with adjustable arm for candles; on splayed tripod
support.   *Height, 47 inches.*

167. MAHOGANY LOWBOY   *English, XVIII Century*

Oblong cyma-molded top; the arched kneehole underframing fitted
with one long drawer and two small drawers, trimmed with bail
handles; supported on angular legs.
      Height, 28 inches; length, 29½ inches.

168. HEPPLEWHITE MAHOGANY LIBRARY TABLE
                    English, XVIII Century

Rectangular molded top, having insert of finely tooled brown
leather. The underframing fitted with six cock-beaded drawers
with bail handles, three at either end. Enriched with a delicate
astragal molding. Supported on four tapering quadrangular legs.
      Height, 31 inches; length, 42 inches.

169. KINGWOOD AND TULIPWOOD COMMODE MOUNTED IN CUIVRE DORÉ
                    Louis XV Period

Curvilinear contour; the *bombé* front fitted with two drawers, and
having a serpentined valance, on incurving tapering legs; the whole
enriched with *cuivre doré* mountings of rocaille motifs. *Brèche
violette* marble top.   *Height, 33 inches; length, 37½ inches.*

170. WALNUT AND OAK SIDE TABLE   *English, XVII Century*

Rectangular molded top; the box frieze fitted with one drawer; supported on balustered legs with a curious H-stretcher.
      Height, 28 inches; length, 28 inches.

171. INLAID WALNUT SIDE TABLE   *English, XVIII Century*

Oblong molded top, cleft at the front corners; the frieze drawer
with pear-drop handles; on round tapering legs, pad feet.
      Height, 28½ inches; length, 32½ inches.

172. CARVED WALNUT PRIE-DIEU   *Italian Renaissance*
Oblong molded top, having notched cornice molding; the front fitted with paneled frieze drawer and a central cupboard door of burl walnut, flanked by grotesque mask pilaster blocks and caryatid pilasters, beneath which is the kneeling box on embryonic claw feet.

Height, 35 inches; width, 28 inches.

173. OAK GATE-LEG TABLE   *English, XVII Century*
Circular top, with two folding flaps; the underframing containing small drawer; on vase-balustered and ring-turned legs and gates.

Height, 30 inches; diameter, extended, 32½ inches.

174. HEPPLEWHITE MAHOGANY KNEEHOLE WRITING-DESK
      English, XVIII Century
Rectangular molded top, reeded at the edges and having an insert of tooled leather and adjustable mirror; the front fitted with nine drawers and a central concave paneled door. Trimmed with chased brass ring handles.

Height, 31 inches; length, 39½ inches.

175. INLAID MAHOGANY CABINET SIDEBOARD   *Sheraton Period*
Oblong hinged top having chamfered corners, the cornice molding vertically inlaid with sycamore; opening and forming with unusual construction a sideboard, extending and having two shelves. The front fitted with two small frieze drawers and double enclosing doors inlaid and exhibiting shell motifs. On stump feet.

Height, 33½ inches; length, 42 inches.

176. WALNUT AND MARQUETERIE CENTRE TABLE
      William and Mary Period
Oblong molded top, enriched with a scrolled oval medallion exhibiting a jardinière of flowers, centring a bird in full song; in the spandrels are sprays of flowers; box frieze with one drawer. On spiraled and knopped legs braced by an X-stretcher, bun feet.

Height, 29½ inches; length, 40 inches.

177. SHERATON INLAID SATINWOOD SEGMENTAL COMMODE
      English, XVIII Century
Semicircular top, inlaid with rosewood, hollywood and sycamore, enriched by a central fan motif, interlacing scrolls and torchères; the frieze with festoons of pendent husks; beneath are double enclosing doors having oval patera surrounded by scrolled leafage and chains of fuchsia drops. Supported by four short quadrangular legs.

Height, 36 inches; length, 60 inches.

178. SHERATON INLAID SATINWOOD OVAL TABLE
English, XVIII Century

Oval top, with tooled leather inset: the underframe fitted with two end drawers; on square tapering legs. Banded and cross-banded with harewood inlay.

Height, 29½ inches; length, 35 inches.

179. SHERATON INLAID SATINWOOD OVAL TABLE
English, XVIII Century

Similar to the preceding.

180. CARVED OAK CHEST
Jacobean Period

Oblong molded and paneled hinged top: the front enriched by a floriated lunetted frieze and central panel carved to a cruciform motif composed of tulip forms: the stiles continuing as supports.

Height, 27 inches; length, 45½ inches.

181. HEPPLEWHITE NEEDLEPOINT MAHOGANY WINDOW SEAT
English, XVIII Century

Rectangular seat with outcurving, scrolled arm-rests: covered in fine needlepoint; the field of *point d'Hongrie* exhibiting a floral design in *petit point*, on four fillet-molded square legs.

Height, 31 inches; length, 45 inches.

182. HEPPLEWHITE MAHOGANY SETTEE
English, XVIII Century

Closed serpentined back, arms and seat covered in deep crimson cut velvet: supported by six slender slightly cabriole legs with leaf-molded knees and feet resembling dolphins' heads.

Height, 38 inches; length, 59 inches.

183. MAHOGANY BUREAU-DESK MOUNTED IN CUIVRE DORÉ
English, XVIII Century

Oblong top: the fall-front opening to interior fitted with numerous drawers and three small cupboard doors: beneath are two small and three long cock-beaded drawers, trimmed with *cuivre doré* leaf handles. On bracket feet.

Height, 45½ inches; width, 42 inches.

184. EMBROIDERED SILK MAHOGANY LOVE SEAT
English, XVIII Century

The square back, seat and wings covered in blue embroidery: supported on graceful slightly cabriole legs with pad feet, connected by an unusual incurving reeded stretcher centring a double X-motif. (Stretcher restored.)

Height, 45½ inches; width, 41 inches.

185. SHERATON INLAID MAHOGANY SIDEBOARD

English, XVIII Century

Oblong: the bow front fitted with central shallow drawer over an arched valance and flanked by an almost square drawer and a cupboard door; trimmed with lion mask handles and enriched within the spandrels by a fan motif. On tapered angular legs.

Height, 36 inches; length, 54 inches.

(*Illustrated*)

186. UPHOLSTERED EASY SETTEE

Rectilinear contour, with slightly canted back and loose cushions; covered in old-blue floriated brocatelle, trimmed with old-gold and blue tasseled fringe: on mahogany short legs.

Height, 31 inches; length, 53 inches.

187. ADAM MAHOGANY ARMCHAIR   *English, XVIII Century*

Of curvilinear contour. Covered in mulberry-crimson velours. The framework fillet-molded: cabriole legs. Studded with bronze nails.

188. SET OF TEN HEPPLEWHITE MAHOGANY DINING-ROOM CHAIRS
English, XVIII Century

Slightly tapering square back and lunette-shaped seat, enriched by an astragal molding; on tapered fluted and quilled square legs with spade feet. Covered in crimson damask.

189. CARVED WALNUT CABINET   *French, François I Period*

In two sections. Oblong top: the front with double enclosing paneled doors carved in bas-relief depicting classically draped figures flanked by engaged columns having capitals of Doric form: beneath is a drawer with a central winged mask. Open below, and supported by swelling columns. Molded plinth.

Height, 55½ inches; width, 43 inches.

190. MAHOGANY EXTENSION DINING-TABLE   *English, XIX Century*

Oblong molded top, with rounded corners: box frieze: supported by round tapering reeded legs. Three extension leaves.

Height, 28½ inches; length, 60 inches.

191. LOUIS XIV NEEDLEPOINT SOFA

Rectangular back, and seat with three loose cushions; on molded stump feet. Covered in eighteenth century needlepoint of brilliant coloring, exhibiting within cartouched framing gaily plumaged peacocks, jardinières of flowers and foliage, in *gros* and *petit point*.

Height, 2 feet 8½ inches; length, 6 feet 9 inches.

192. CARVED OAK COURT CUPBOARD   *Jacobean Period*

Rectangular molded soffited top; the frieze flat-carved with a scroll motif and having turned pendants: the recessed front fitted with three cupboard doors deeply molded and carved: the lower section with strap-work frieze, and two large paneled double doors.

Height, 5 feet 4 inches; width, 4 feet 9 inches.

193. GREEN LAQUÉ AND PARCEL-GILDED CONSOLE TABLE
Venetian, XVIII Century

Rectangular: the box frieze enriched with a carved and gilded floral motif flanked by paterae. Supported at the front on canalated columns with Composite capitals. *Brèche blanche* marble top.

Height, 36½ inches; length, 50 inches.

36

194. QUEEN ANNE WALNUT ARMCHAIR   *English, XVIII Century*
Open square back, with swept whorl top rail and interlacing scroll
—splat; longitudinally curved and voluted arms. On quadrangular
box stretchered legs. Slip seat in green damask.

195. NEEDLEPOINT MAHOGANY WING CHAIR

English, XVIII Century
—Serpentined oblong back, wings and outscrolling arms covered in
brilliantly colored needlepoint displaying fruit and flowers; on quadrangular stretchered legs.

196. CARVED MAHOGANY CONSOLE TABLE   *Chippendale Style*
Massive oblong top; box frieze enriched by a fretted motif. Supported by four bracketed angular legs developing the same motif;
block feet.

Height, 32½ inches; length, 59 inches.

197. SET OF SIX CARVED WALNUT SIDE CHAIRS   *James II Period*
Tapered baluster uprights and scrolled arch cresting, approximately
square seat which, with the back, is *canné;* turned and block stretchered legs with hooped frontal stretcher.

198. TWO NEEDLEPOINT MAHOGANY ARMCHAIRS

English, XVIII Century
Slightly canted oblong back; scrolled and voluted splayed arms with
arm-pads join the shaped seat-rail back from the front legs, which
are cabrioles, terminating in leaf-scrolled feet. Covered in *petit* and
gros point developing rustic scenes in harmonious reds, blues, greens
and ivory on a black ground.

199. CARVED WALNUT REFECTORY TABLE BENCH

Italian, XVI Century
Rectangular molded top; the interestingly carved valance centring
an escutcheon charged with a Medici armorial insignia. On splayed
lyre-shaped end supports.

Height, 1 foot 8½ inches; length, 7 feet 2 inches.

200. CHINESE CHIPPENDALE MAHOGANY DOUBLE-ENDED SEAT

English, XVIII Century
Of unusual length. The seat and outcurving ends in the original
blue Spitalfields damask; supported by six quadrangular stretchered
legs carved to a latticed design.

Height, 2 feet 6 inches; length, 7 feet 10 inches.

37

201. OAK REFECTORY TABLE BENCH   *Jacobean Period*
    Oblong molded top, with box frieze: on simple balustered and
26.—stretchered legs.

Height, 1 foot 11 inches; length, 5 feet 11 inches.

202. BRUSSELS RENAISSANCE TAPESTRY WALNUT SETTEE
    Oblong canted back and flaring outscrolling arms. supported on
blocked and turned stretchered legs. with elaborate hooped frontal
stretchers. Covered in fine Renaissance tapestry. the back depicting
a palace of fine architectural construction, with open arcaded wings;
the loose seat cushion and arms in conventional foliage. (Frame of
a later date.)

Height, 3 feet 2 inches; length, 6 feet 5 inches.

203

203. BRUSSELS RENAISSANCE TAPESTRY WALNUT SETTEE
    Similar to the preceding: with variation in design of tapestry, the
back exhibiting an animated hunting scene.

Height, 3 feet 2 inches; length, 6 feet 5 inches.

(*Illustrated*)

38

204. CARVED OAK COURT CUPBOARD — *Flemish, XVII Century*
Rectangular molded top, with double enclosing paneled doors
flanked by spiraled half columns and capped by leaf-carved pilaster
blocks; beneath is a deep cyma-curved molding opening as a drawer
and double doors similar to those of the upper section.

Height, 5 feet 2½ inches; width, 4 feet 8 inches.

205. ENGLISH CRIMSON VELVET CARVED WALNUT SETTEE
Double-arched high back, wings, outscrolling arms and seat covered
in fine old crimson velvet: the back having a central panel of Renaissance gold-embroidered velvet: the whole banded in gold galloon.
Supported on five cabriole legs, the front three being finely carved
and terminatng in claw-and-ball feet; the seat rail enriched with inlaid concave shells. Loose seat cushion. (Frame of a later date.)

Height, 4 feet 7 inches; length, 5 feet.

206. INLAID WALNUT SECRETARY BOOKCASE — *Queen Anne Period*
In two sections. Oblong molded top with concave cornice molding;
supported by fluted and quilled pilasters enclosing glazed door. The
lower section having slant-front opening to fitted interior: beneath
are two end-on drawers and two long drawers enriched with recticu-
lated brasses and bail handles. On bracket feet. (The six small
drawers of the interior are reconstructed.)

Height, 6 feet 5 inches; width, 2 feet 5 inches.

207. PAIR BRONZE TORCHÈRES — *Italian, XVI Century*
Massive baluster stem, on splayed circular foot. Fitted for electricity.

Total height, 6 feet.

208. CARVED OAK CUPBOARD HUTCH — *English, circa 1520*
Rectangular tall hutch: the front fitted with eleven cupboard doors
finely flat-carved, exhibiting foliated lozenge, quatrefoil, trefoil and
other motifs; wrought iron hinges.

Height, 6 feet; width, 5 feet 1 inch.

209. TWO GILDED METAL STANDARD LANTERNS
Venetian, XVIII Century
Trilateral glazed body, with domed top having five conical finials.
Supported by bamboo stems. Fitted for electricity.

Height, 6 feet 10 inches.

39

210. IMPORTANT INLAID WALNUT SECRETARY

Early Queen Anne. Period

In two sections. Hooded molded top; the frieze fitted with two end-on drawers; the fall-front inlaid with a series of cyma-curves, opening to fitted interior having numerous drawers, pigeon-holes and a central cupboard. Lower section with two small and two long drawers; on bracket feet. Trimmed with cruciform brasses, drop-handles and pierced escutcheons.

Height, 6 feet 6 inches; width, 3 feet 5 inches.

Note: Illustrated in G. L. Hunter's *Decorative Furniture*, page 346.

(Illustrated)

211. THREEFOLD PAINTED CORDOVA LEATHER SCREEN

Spanish, XVIII Century

Oblong serpentined panels, exhibiting on a deep old-gold field entwined naturalistic hibiscus, tulips, pomegranates, fuchsias and foliage. *Height, 6 feet 11 inches; width, 6 feet 8½ inches.*

212. SHERATON INLAID SATINWOOD SECRETARY CABINET

English, XVIII Century

Tall cabinet in two sections, of rectilinear contour; the top with double glazed doors, flanked by tapering columns in relief, pencil-lined with rosewood inlay. Lower section with pull-down front, supported by quadrants; opening to interior fitted with three drawers having ivory knop handles; beneath are double enclosing doors, similarly flanked; the whole banded and cross banded in darker colored inlay. *Height, 7 feet 8 inches; width, 2 feet 6 inches.*

213. SHERATON MAHOGANY CHINA CABINET

English, XVIII Century

Rectangular cyma-curved top, with a dentil and lanceolate cornice molding; the front fitted with double enclosing doors which with the sides are glazed and traceried, having reeded moldings; on enclosed base. Fitted with three mahogany and three glass shelves, and lined with crimson damask. *Height, 8 feet 9 inches; width, 4 feet 2 inches.*

214. HEPPLEWHITE UPHOLSTERED PAINTED SETTEE

English, XVIII Century

Rectilinear, with one loose seat, three back and two side cushions covered in amethyst brocatelle, developing a large palmate design; supported by eight short tapered square legs.

Height, 2 feet 10 inches; length, 7 feet.

No. 210. IMPORTANT INLAID WALNUT SECRETARY
(*Early Queen Anne Period*)

41

215. HEPPLEWHITE MAHOGANY SETTEE *English, XVIII Century*
Arched back, outscrolling arms and slightly bow seat, covered in crimson damask exhibiting a fine *Louis* Quinze design. On six quadrangular fillet-molded stretchered legs.

Height, 2 feet 10 inches; length, 7 feet.

216. OAK REFECTORY TABLE *Jacobean Period*
Massive rectangular top of unusual length; shaped underframe. Supported by six columnar box stretchered legs.

Height, 2 feet 7 inches; width, 2 feet 6 inches; length, 11 feet 3 inches.

217. POWDER-BLUE FLORAL DAMASK SOFA
Oblong back, seat and closed arms covered in fine eighteenth century damask; banded with broad gold and blue galloon and trimmed with deep fringe having gold tassels. Three loose cushions.

Height, 2 feet 9½ inches; length, 6 feet 7 inches.

218. CHIPPENDALE MAHOGANY DROP-LEAP DINING TABLE
English, XVIII Century
Oval top, with leaf-carved edges and having two rule-jointed leaves; supported by eight quadrangular legs, four of which are adjustable.

Height, 2 feet 4½ inches; width, 4 feet 8 inches; length, 8 feet 1 inch.

219. TWO GILDED METAL STANDARD LANTERNS
Venetian, XVII Century
Hexagonal glazed body, with six carvatid pilasters; the bossed dome surmounted by a pennant bearing the *Lion* of Saint Mark; supported by a crimson painted shaft. Siena marble base.

Height, 9 feet 5 inches

END OF FIRST SESSION

SECOND SESSION

THURSDAY, MAY 6, AT 2:15 P. M

Catalogue Numbers 220 to 423 Inclusive

220. BRONZE INKSTAND   *Florentine, XVI Century*

Cauldron-shape: supported by three coroneted eagles adorsed, with wings outspread.

Height, 3½ inches.

221. BRONZE INKSTAND WITH COVER   *Italian, XVI Century*

Circular bowl, supported by three harpies: the domed cover with erect winged cherub supporting a shield at his side. The bowl and cover are by different artists of the sixteenth century.

Height, 8 inches.

222. PAIR BRONZE CANDLESTICKS   *In the manner of Sansovino*

Urn-shaped *bobèche,* with lobed circular grease tray; on domed tripod support embodying three angel masks.

Height, 7 inches

223. CRIMSON VELVET PHOTOGRAPH FRAME

Rectangular molded frame, covered in rich Renaissance velvet and banded with gold galloon: the interior and exterior with crimson damask.

Height, 12½ inches; width, 11 inches.

224. CRIMSON VELVET PHOTOGRAPH FRAME

Rectangular molded frame, covered in rich Renaissance velvet and banded with gold galloon: the interior and exterior with crimson damask.

Height, 12¾ inches; width, 11 inches.

225. CUT VELVET PHOTOGRAPH FRAME

Rectangular frame, covered in fine *drap d'or* rose-crimson Renaissance cut velvet: the back in golden-yellow damask.

Height, 15½ inches; width, 12½ inches.

226. AMETHYST VELVET AND BROCATELLE BOUDOIR BOX

Oblong, with removable cover. In fine amethyst brocatelle and banded with silver galloon; the sides with old velvet.

Height, 3¾ inches; length, 8½ inches

43

227. CRIMSON VELVET AND NEEDLEPAINTED LIBRARY DESK SET
Comprising rectangular photograph frame, oblong stationery box, folding blotter and desk tray. The tray with ogival arched top and outset rounded corners: the oblong box with circular Renaissance gold-embroidered medallion depicting a saintly figure.

228. NEEDLEPAINTED DAMASK BOUDOIR DESK SET
Comprising photograph frame, folding blotter and desk tray. Covered in *bleu de ciel* damask, enriched with floral motifs in fine needlepoint. Banded with silver galloon.

229. EMBROIDERED CUT VELVET PHOTOGRAPH FRAME
Rectangular frame, covered in fine old rose-crimson cut velvet embroidered in ivory silk. *Height, 15¼ inches; width, 12½ inches.*

230. NEEDLEPAINTED DESK BOX
Rectangular, with removable top covered in old Italian gold-embroidered silk and banded with gold galloon: the sides in crimson damask. *Height, 3¼ inches; length, 9 inches.*

231. SILK BROCADE PHOTOGRAPH FRAME
Rectangular frame, covered in fine old rose-crimson floral brocade. *Height, 15 inches; width, 12 inches.*

232. RENAISSANCE NEEDLEPAINTED DESK BOX
Rectangular, with segmental arched top: the front displaying in fine needlepoint a depiction of OUR LORD; banded in gold galloon and the sides in gold and rose-crimson damask. *Height, 7½ inches; length, 11¾ inches.*

233. RENAISSANCE NEEDLEPAINTED DESK BOX
Oblong, with removable top covered in fine gold-embroidered silk depicting a façade, bearing the arms of the Medici family; the sides in crimson velvet. *Height, 2¼ inches; length, 9 inches.*

234. ROSE-CRIMSON AND GOLD BROCADE PHOTOGRAPH FRAME
Rectangular frame, covered in fine old French brocade and banded with scalloped silver galloon. Back and interior lined with damask. *Height, 12½ inches; width, 11 inches.*

235. GOLD-EMBROIDERED SILK DESK BOX
Oblong, with removable top enriched with fine Renaissance panel of gold-embroidered crimson silk, exhibiting a central rosette flanked by scrolled dolphins: the sides in crimson damask. *Height, 4 inches; length, 12½ inches.*

236. CRIMSON VELVET PHOTOGRAPH FRAME
Rectangular cyma-molded frame, covered in fine old velvet and banded with silver galloon; the back in crimson damask.
Height, 15 inches; width, 12 inches.

237. CRIMSON VELVET PHOTOGRAPH FRAME
Rectangular molded frame, covered in rich Renaissance velvet and banded with gold galloon; the interior and exterior with crimson damask.
Height, 15 inches; width, 12 inches.

238. RENAISSANCE NEEDLEPAINTED DESK BOX
Oblong, with removable top covered in fine gold-embroidered silk depicting a façade, bearing the arms of the Medici family; the sides in crimson velvet.
Height, 2¼ inches; length, 7½ inches.

239. BRONZE INKSTAND   *Italian Renaissance*
Cauldron-shape; enriched with festoons of flowers and drapery, supported by three seated putti.
Height, 3½ inches.

240. TURQUOISE-BLUE BOWL   *K'ang-hsi*
Circular shallow bowl, with incurving neck; two scrolled handles. Beautiful glaze.
Diameter, 5½ inches.

241. SMALL DECORATED PORCELAIN BOWL   *K'ang-hsi*
Pale *café au lait*, with spray of chrysanthemum and prunus branches; the interior glazed in creamy-white. Gilded silver mounts.
Diameter, 5½ inches.

242. CARVED JADE TWO-HANDLED COVERED COUPE   *Ming*
Bell-shaped, with carved teakwood cover having jade bird finial; animalistic scroll handles. The body carved with intricate ornamentation. On teakwood stand.
Length, 5½ inches.

243. BOW PORCELAIN FIGURINE   *English, XVIII Century*
Figure of a child draped in an apple-green mantle, seated upon the bough of a tree.
Height, 6 inches.

244. PAIR FAMILLE ROSE VASES   *Ch'ien-lung*
Small beaker-shape, with outcurving lobed lip; decorated with floral motifs.
Height, 6 inches.

245. PAIR ROSE DU BARRY JARDINIÈRES   *Minton, XVIII Century*
Deep bowl-shape, with shell handles; on circular foot. The reserved
medallions exhibiting on a white ground richly painted flower scenes;
the whole enhanced with gilding.

Height, 6 inches.

246. TWO CHELSEA DECORATED PORCELAIN VASES
English, XVIII Century
Decorated with oval medallions representing birds with gaily col-
ored plumage; pierced top on scroll base.

Height, 8½ inches.

247. PAIR DECORATED PORCELAIN TWO-HANDLED VASES
Crown Derby, XVIII Century
Urn-shape, with scroll handles, on circular foot and square plinth,
the white ground exhibiting sprays of flowers, the reserves in royal-
blue.

Height, 8½ inches.

248. PAIR DECORATED PORCELAIN TWO-HANDLED VASES
Crown Derby, XVIII Century
Similar to the preceding. (One handle damaged.)

249. SET OF THREE CHELSEA VASES   *XVIII Century*
Quadrilateral tapered body, with polygonal domed top; enriched
with massed sprays of buds in relief; bearing red anchor mark at
base.

Height of two, 8 inches; of the other, 9½ inches.

250. TWO FINE GOLD ANCHOR MARK CHELSEA VASES
English, XVIII Century
Decorated with pheasants and other exotic birds with brightly
colored plumage; scroll shaped handles.

Height, 11 inches.

251. DECORATED PORCELAIN GARNITURE
Chamberlains, Worcester, XVIII Century
Comprising flower-holder and two covered vases, in canary-yellow
enriched with gilding; reserved in monotone are old English rural
scenes. (One cover damaged.)

Heights, 6 and 7 inches.

252. PAIR BLUE AND WHITE VASES   *K'ang-hsi*
Oviform, with incurving neck and domed circular foot; cream-white
glaze decorated in soft tone of cobalt-blue exhibiting conventional
foliage.

Height, 8½ inches.

253. FAMILLE VERTE ROSE BOWL   *K'ang-hsi*

Fine blue-white glaze; the interior and exterior richly decorated with *chinoiserie* motifs.

Diameter, 8½ inches.

254. CASTEL DURANTE MAJOLICA EWER   *XVII Century*

Pear-shaped, with upturned short spout and strap loop handle; inscribed at the back: MEL-ROSATSO; at the front with date 1694. In fine enameled blues, greens and golden-yellows.

Height, 8¼ inches.

255. PORCELAIN FIGURINE   *Chelsea Derby, XVIII Century*

Erect winged semi-draped figure poised by a flowering shrub; on rocaille base, enriched with gilding.

Height, 9 inches.

256. FAMILLE VERTE PLAQUE   *K'ang-hsi*

In the finely enameled colors of the *famille verte*, depicting a mandarin standing before a table with animated figures in the foreground.

Diameter, 15 inches.

257. TWO CHINESE LOWESTOFT FOUR-SIDED VASES AND COVERS

Each side decorated with Chinese figures, in brightly colored costumes; the covers surmounted by kylins.

Height, 17 inches.

258. FAMILLE VERTE COVERED JAR   *K'ang-hsi*

Oviform, with dome cover; *ju-i* form panels reserved in a brilliant green exhibiting fishes and floral motifs, on a *rouge-de-fer* diapered ground, the base enriched with a banding in a similar color composition.

Height, 13½ inches.

259. PAIR CHINESE LOWESTOFT COVERED VASES   *XVIII Century*

Ovoidal, with domed cover having dog Fu finial; ivory-white ground with four medallions reserved in white, depicting naturalistic flowers and butterflies.

Height, 12¼ inches.

260. PAIR FAMILLE VERTE POTPOURRI BOWLS AND COVERS

K'ang-hsi

Deep bowl, with domed cover and gilded bronze cone finial; richly decorated with chrysanthemums and other floral motifs in characteristic colors of the *famille verte*. (One cover restored.)

Height, 10 inches.

From the Collection of the late Lord Brassey, Battle Abbey.

47

261. Two Chinese Lowestoft Jardinières   *XVIII Century*

Square, the sides enriched with panels exhibiting baskets of brightly colored flowers and small floral bouquets surrounded by a turquoise-blue border.

Height, 16 inches.

262. Pair Decorated Porcelain Candlesticks

Bow, XVIII Century

Upon a rocky base the sea god Poseidon is standing by a dolphin supporting another upon his shoulder emitting a *bobèche* for a candle. On fine Louis Quinze base.

Height, 14¾ inches.

(*Illustrated*)

263. Pair Blue and White Hawthorn Ginger Jars   *K'ang-hsi*

Oviform; finely glazed cobalt-blue, displaying sprays of prunus blossoms in white; in the *ju-i* head reserves are flying dragons. With teakwood stands and covers. (One cover damaged.)

Height, 10½ inches.

264. DECORATED PORCELAIN GROUP   *Chelsea, XVIII Century*

Beautifully modeled winged figure of Time with scythe, standing on a rocky base, supporting on his left arm a rocaille receptacle for a small clock or watch; at the left is a seated figure of Youth. (One wing damaged.)

Height, 15 inches.

265. SANG-DE-BOEUF OVIFORM VASE   *Tao Kuang*

Pear-shape, with cylindrical neck; brilliant glaze of dense ox-blood quality, shading to a fine light green.

Height, 15 inches.

266. LOWESTOFT BOWL   *XVIII Century*

Circular: decorated in the Chinese manner, the interior with a medallioned Eastern figure, the exterior with naturalistic flowers.

Diameter, 10 inches.

267. DECORATED PORCELAIN BOWL   *Ch'ien-lung*

Circular: the exterior in fine mazarine-blue, the reserved panels depicting flowers and birds, in *rouge de fer* and fine green.

Diameter, 10 inches.

268. BLUE AND WHITE PORCELAIN VASE   *K'ang-hsi*

Cylindrical, with tapering collared neck and expanding lip, exhibiting *chinoiserie* scenes. (Slight crack at shoulder.)

Height, 18 inches.

269. CHAMBERLAIN WORCESTER DESSERT SERVICE
     English, XVIII Century

Comprising: Seventeen dessert plates, two shell-shaped fruit dishes, two oval and two square fruit dishes and one compotier. Decorated with naturalistic sprays of flowers, the marli enriched with scrolled leafage in gold.

270. DECORATED PORCELAIN VASE   *Ch'ien-lung*

Oviform, with high cylindrical neck: decorated on a gray-blue ground with *chinoiserie* motifs in golden-browns, greens and white: fine crackle.

Height, 26½ inches.

271. TWO FAMILLE VERTE PLAQUES   *K'ang-hsi*

Circular deep plate: the cavetto with garden scenes: the marli with dwarf plants and scrolled cartouches. In finely enameled colors of the *famille verte*.

Diameter, 15 inches.

272. PAIR LARGE POWDER-BLUE JARDINIÈRES   *K'ang-hsi*

Ovo-cylindrical, with flanged lip; glazed in fine fluctuating tones deepening to darker areas. On elaborately carved and molded teakwood stand with hexagonal base.

Height, 16 inches; diameter. 20¾ inches; height of stand, 25 inches.

(*Illustrated*)

273. GLAZED POTTERY PLAQUE   *English, dated* 1542

Rare plate, glazed yellow upon a brown ground; the deep cavetto exhibiting in relief the figure of Saint Catherine of Alexandria within a laurel wreath, glazed green: the marli enriched with an arabesqued palmate motif. (Repaired.)

Diameter, 13½ inches.

274. BISQUE MANTLE CLOCK MOUNTED IN CUIVRE DORÉ

Louis Seize Period

Circular dial in architectural setting: at the right an erect classically draped female figure, at the left a kneeling cupidon with a quiver of arrows: on oval base with a banding of ormolu, having an astragal molding: on ball feet.

Height, 12¼ inches; width. 10½ inches.

50

275. BLUE AND WHITE VASE   *K'ang-hsi*
Double-aster-shape; tall incurving neck with two lizard handles, decorated with an allover patterning of foliage and chrysanthemums.
Height, 17 inches.

276. HISPANO-MORESQUE LUSTRED PLAQUE   *XV Century*
Circular, with deep cavetto and upcurving rim; decorated with a geometrical design. Fine golden lustre.
Diameter, 12¾ inches.

277. HISPANO-MORESQUE LUSTRED PLAQUE   *XVI Century*
Circular, with embossed *tondo;* the *tondino* and flaring rim enriched with conventionalized flowers and leafage outlined in cobalt-blue. Rich gold lustre.
Diameter, 15½ inches.

278. HISPANO-MORESQUE LUSTRED PLAQUE   *Late XVI Century*
Circular; the cavetto depicting a charming rendition of THE CORONATION OF THE VIRGIN MOTHER: the marli with a diaper motif. Fine golden lustre.
Diameter, 20 inches.

279. DECORATED PORCELAIN TEA SERVICE
Lowestoft, XVIII Century
Comprising: Teapot, ten tea- and three coffee-cups, eight saucers, two confiture dishes, one basin, one hot-milk pitcher, and a small covered vase. Decorated in the oriental manner, with jardinières of flowers and other motifs. (The vase slightly damaged.)

TEXTILES

280. JADE-GREEN VELVET BOUDOIR DESK SET
(A) Rectangular cyma-molded photograph frame. (B) Oblong box: enriched with a needlepainted medallion depicting a mitred bishop. (C) Folding blotter; enriched with a gold-embroidered floral motif. (D) Rectangular compartmented desk tray with ogival arched back. Banded in silver galloon.

281. NEEDLEPOINT CHAIR SEAT AND BACK   *Queen Anne Period*
Depicting on a golden-brown field in fine needlepoint, roses, tulips and fine leafage in shaded reds, variegated blues and greens.

51

282. VENETIAN BROCADE BOUDOIR DESK SET

Comprising rectangular photograph frame and folding blotter, pair book-ends and desk tray. Covered in fine old floral brocade, banded with gold galloon.

283. NEEDLEPAINTED AND CRIMSON DAMASK DESK BOX

Oblong, with removable top covered in crimson silk damask enriched by an Italian Renaissance needlepainted medallion depicting St. Paul and having at the edges S-scrolling in gold thread.

Height, 4¼ inches; length, 12 inches.

284.   285

284. TAPESTRY CUSHION   *Flemish Renaissance*

Square; portraying within a medallion, the seated figure of Our Lord with eight holy women before the temple, in attitudes of devotion. Border of foliage in colors of variegated reds, blues, greens and browns on an écru ground. Green damask back. Trimmed with crimson ball fringe.

(*Illustrated*)

285. GROS AND PETIT POINT CUSHION   *English, XVIII Century*

Approximately square; the central medallion depicting a mandarin and his attendant before a conventional cypress tree. Dated 1725.

(*Illustrated*)

52

286. NEEDLEPOINT CUSHION English, XVIII Century
Square; depicting within a scrolled cartouche mystical scene in the Chinese manner. Trimmed with ball fringe.

287. NEEDLEPOINT CUSHION English, XVIII Century
Square; depicting within a central medallion of fine *petit point* in the Chinese manner, a seated female figure with an attendant maid at the punka flanked by cypress trees.

288. EMBROIDERED VELVET AND BROCATELLE CUSHION
Italian Renaissance
Oblong; the central panel in moss-green velvet depicting a central medallion with saintly figure. Trimmed with a tassel at each corner.

289. PAIR NEEDLEPOINT CUSHIONS Italian Renaissance
Oblong; with gold-embroidered panel banded with gold galloon. enclosing central medallion depicting saintly figures. Trimmed with ball fringe.

290. RENAISSANCE NEEDLEPAINTED CRIMSON VELVET DESK SET
(A) Segmental arched stationery box, portraying in fine colors a depiction of Our Lord in the attitude of benediction. (B) Serpentined arched folding blotter, depicting in superb needlepoint a Virgin Martyr. Lined with crimson and gold brocatelle.

291. TAPESTRY CUSHION Flemish Renaissance
Square; depicting at the centre a scrolled escutcheon with the armorial bearings of a Flemish gentleman amidst fruit, flowers and birds. Inscribed on the banderolle: V. AMLVNXEN. In fine colors of variegated greens, blues, golden-yellows, reds, browns, fawn and ivory. Green silk back. Trimmed with tufted fringe.

292. RENAISSANCE CRIMSON APPLIQUÉ VELVET DESK BOX
Rectangular, with segmental arched cover. In fine old rose-crimson velvet appliqué with embroidered silk, displaying conventional leaf design.
Height, 7 inches; length, 12 inches.

293. JADE-GREEN DAMASK PHOTOGRAPH FRAME AND PAIR BOOK-ENDS
Rectangular molded frame, covered in fine old green floral damask and banded with gold galloon. With matching book-ends.
Height of frame, 15½ inches; width, 13 inches.

294. JADE-GREEN DAMASK PHOTOGRAPH FRAME AND PAIR BOOK-ENDS
Rectangular frame, covered in fine old green floral damask and
banded with gold galloon. With matching book-ends.
Height of frame, 15½ inches; width, 13 inches.

295. TAPESTRY CUSHION   *Flemish Renaissance*
Oblong; depicting within a fruit and floral medallion the coat of
arms and mantlings of a Flemish burgomaster, inscribed upon the
banderolle: V. OPPERSHAUSEN. With green silk back. Trimmed
with green tufted fringe.

296. TAPESTRY CUSHION   *Flemish Renaissance*
Oblong; depicting within a fruit and floral medallion the coat of
arms and mantlings of a Flemish burgomaster, inscribed upon the
banderolle: V. HEIMBORCH. The back in green silk. Trimmed with
green tufted fringe.

297. CRIMSON VELVET AND GOLD-EMBROIDERED CUSHION
                                          Italian Renaissance
Square; the central panel with gold embroidery depicting within a
circular medallion, THE MADONNA AND CHILD. Crimson silk back.
Trimmed with short fringe.

298. NEEDLEPOINT PANEL   *French Renaissance*
Portraying in a wooded landscape, a seated male figure beneath a
canopy; at the left are two female, at the right two male figures.
Inscribed at the base: IVOIT HOLOFERNUS. Framed.
Height, 20 inches; length, 25 inches.

299. FRAMED RENAISSANCE TAPESTRY PANEL *Flemish, XVI Century*
Within an arch composed of grotesque figures, classic urns and
suspended drapery, is the seated figure of the Madonna, hooded
and robed in a fluctuating blue tunic and crimson mantle, reading
from the open missal supported by her left hand; she holds a cross
in her right. Vista of primitive landscape. Mounted on crimson
velvet.
Height, 25 inches; width, 22½ inches.

300. GOLD-EMBROIDERED GREEN BROCATELLE CUSHION
                                          Italian Renaissance
Oblong; the central panel depicting a beautifully needlepainted rendition of St. Andrew. Trimmed with green ball fringe.

54

301. GOLD-EMBROIDERED AND BRO-
CATELLE CUSHION
180.—   *Italian Gothic Period*
Square; with central panel finely embroidered in gold and
silken threads, depicting saintly
figure. Trimmed with fringe.

(*Illustrated*)

301

302. CRIMSON VELVET AND GOLD-
EMBROIDERED COVER
150.—   *Italian Renaissance*
Fine crimson velvet with gold embroidery, displaying at the ends
and border a scroll and floral motif. Deep fringe.

Length, 7 feet 3 inches; width, 36 inches.

303. NEEDLEWORK PANEL   *Louis Seize Period*
Green-blue ground exhibiting bouquets of naturalistic roses, border
20.— of ribbon entwined with rose-buds.

Length, 56 inches; width, 24 inches.

304. OBLONG TAPESTRY PANEL   *Flemish Renaissance*
Central cartouche with figures before a wooded landscape, flanked
10.— by telamons supporting bouquets of flowers. Woven in fine colors.

Height, 19 inches; length, 57 inches.

305. RARE ROSE-CRIMSON QUILTED SILK BED COVER
250.—   *Probably English, Tudor Period*
Rich field, exhibiting in relief a close Tudor design. A central
medallion enclosing a coat of arms embodying the Tudor rose and
bordered by scrolled and voluted branches of roses; Junoesque
figures, cupidons, stag-hounds hunting a stag and other motifs.

Length, 7 feet 9 inches; width, 5 feet 8 inches.

306. EMBROIDERED CRIMSON BANNER   *Italian Renaissance*
The central panel exhibiting within oval medallions, The Virgin
10.— Mother and Child; a Virgin Martyr, and Saint Sebastian flanked by
rich crimson velvet, banded with broad gold galloon; deep fringe.

Height, 56 inches; width, 25 inches.

FURNITURE

307. CARVED MAHOGANY CANTERBURY   *English, XVIII Century*
Rectangular body, fitted with drawer; on turned inverted cup legs;
superimposed by series of bars set saltirewise and joined by spindles
as rests for music and papers.

Height, 20½ inches; width, 20 inches.

308. LOUIS XVI ORMOLU MANTEL CLOCK
Circular white enameled dial; rectangular case chamfered at the
corners; with fluted pilasters and acorn and vase finials; on balustraded marble base.

Height, 12½ inches; width, 7½ inches.

309. TWO ADAM CRYSTAL WALL SCONCES   *English, XVIII Century*
Vase-baluster and lanceolate stem from which radiate three down-
scrolled and two up-scrolled arms, having urn-shaped *bobêches* enriched with chains of sapphire-blue and white crystal drops.

Height, 27 inches; extended, 18½ inches.

310. TWO ADAM CRYSTAL WALL SCONCES   *English, XVIII Century*
Similar to the preceding.

Height, 27 inches; extended, 18½ inches.

311. PAIR WROUGHT IRON ANDIRONS   *Italian Gothic*
Spiraled shaft, with fine cresting of coroneted leafage and vase-
shaped finial; on arched support.

Height, 39½ inches.

312. CUIVRE DORÉ MANTEL CLOCK   *By Deliste Frères, Paris*
Circular dial; in rectangular canalated case, having a vase finial;
draped with festoons of leafage and ribbons. On rectangular guilloche and leaf molded base with marble plinth.

Height, 13¼ inches; width, 7½ inches.

313. BRONZE EQUESTRIAN FIGURE
After Antonio Filarete, Italian, XVIII Century
EMPEROR MARCUS AURELIUS. The noble Roman is seated astride a
very powerful caparisoned charger. He wears a long toga over
simple robes. Mounted on marble plinth.

Height of statue, 14½ inches; base, 8 inches.

314. CARVED OAK JOINT STOOL   *Jacobean Period, circa 1650*
Rectangular molded top; the underframing interestingly carved with
a lunette motif; on turned columnar stretchered legs having an out-
ward spread.

Height, 23½ inches; width, 18 inches.

56

315. MAHOGANY DRESSING TABLE MIRROR *English, XVIII Century*
Rectangular beveled swing mirror; box base having three slightly incurving drawers, trimmed with drop loop handles. Bracket feet.
Height, 21½ inches; width, 15 inches.

316. NEEDLEPOINT MAHOGANY POLE SCREEN *Chippendale Period*
Oblong frame, enclosing panel of fine *gros* and *petit point* display-ing a jardinière emitting naturalistic flowers and foliage; on tripod support enriched with fuchsia motifs.
Height, 46½ inches; width, 20 inches.

317. CHIPPENDALE CARVED AND GILDED MANTEL MIRROR
English, circa 1750
Oblong; richly carved in this master's rusticated style, revealing French inspiration through the rocaille motifs, enclosing at the top a recumbent lion, at the sides boar hounds. In original gilding.
Height, 2 feet 9 inches; length, 5 feet.

318. NEEDLEPOINT CARVED AND GILDED FIRE SCREEN
Louis Seize Period
The arched frame enriched with guilloche and astragal moldings; on splayed supports enclosing superb panel of silk needlepoint, ex-hibiting on an *écru* ground a lyre-shape motif and massed sprays of flowers in greens, reds, golden-yellows, browns and deep blue.
Height, 46½ inches; width, 27 inches.

319. NEEDLEPOINT CARVED WALNUT FAUTEUIL
Italian, XVIII Century
Charming scroll-molded shaped frame, enriched by carved leafage and rosettes; cabriole legs and scrolled leaf feet. Upholstered in *petit point*, depicting in fine colors of écru, blues and reds, a pas-toral scene, and another of birds amid verdure.

320. SHERATON INLAID MAHOGANY CLOCK AND BAROMETER
English, XVIII Century
Banjo-shaped case; fitted below with barometer; above a clock sur-mounted by a thermometer, on either side of which are gilt columns; scrolled cornice.
Height, 48 inches.

321. CARVED OAK MIRROR *Régence Period*
Oblong mirror; the inner molding carved to a cabochon and car-touche motif with key-cornered frame; the pediment latticed and foliated, enriched with a quiver of arrows set saltirewise with a flaming torch.
Height, 4 feet 6½ inches; width, 3 feet 2½ inches.

322. BROCADE KINGWOOD FIRE SCREEN *French, XVIII Century*
—Oblong arched frame, enclosing panel of fine brocade exhibiting on an ivory ground a Louis Seize design in silver threads outlined in crimson; on splayed end supports.

Height, 44 inches; width, 25 inches.

323. MAHOGANY PEMBROKE TABLE *Chippendale Period*
Rectangular top, having two rule-jointed leaves; the frieze fitted with one drawer; supported by angular molded legs, braced by a pierced stretcher set saltirewise.

Height, 28 inches; length extended, 36½ inches.

324. ADAM NEEDLEPOINT CARVED AND GILDED ARMCHAIR
English, XVIII Century
—Molded shaped frame, enriched with anthemion motifs. On tapered fluted legs. Seat, back, and arm-pads covered in fine *petit* and *gros point* of the eighteenth century depicting rustic figures surrounded by conventional foliations; executed in charming colors on a *tête de nègre* ground.

325. SHERATON INLAID SATINWOOD WORK TABLE
English, XVIII Century
Rectangular hinged parqueterie top, inlaid with a floral motif; fitted interior; on fluted baluster legs connected by shelf stretcher.

Height, 29½ inches; width, 17½ inches.

326. ADAM CARVED AND GILDED WALL MIRROR
English, XVIII Century
—Graceful heart-shape, having at the shoulders scrolled acanthus leafage and chains of pendent husks; crested by a ram's-head bearing a volute from which depend chains of fuchsia drops: leaf-carved base.

Height, 57 inches; width, 25½ inches.

327. VIEUX-ROSE BROCADE MAHOGANY FIRE SCREEN
Chippendale Period
—Two folds, enclosing oblong panels of fine brocade; beneath are reticulated arcaded panels of Gothic feeling; on slender spindle legs and stretchers.

Height, 43½ inches; width, 38 inches.

328. INLAID WALNUT LOWBOY *Queen Anne Period*
Oblong molded top: the front fitted with one long drawer and three small drawers. trimmed with *cuivre doré* bail handles composed of festooned flowers: on cabriole legs with pad feet.

Height, 30½ inches; width, 28 inches.

329. TWO CRIMSON VELVET CARVED WALNUT ARMCHAIRS
Italian Renaissance
Open canted back with acanthus leaf carved finials; molded flat arms projecting beyond quadrangular supports which continue as legs braced by side stretchers and having a frontal stretcher reticulated to a geometrical design. Seat and back covered in crimson velvet with appliqué silk galloon; trimmed with deep fringe.

330. TWO CRIMSON VELVET CARVED WALNUT ARMCHAIRS
Italian Renaissance
Similar to the preceding.

331. TWO CARVED WOOD PARCEL-GILDED PEDESTALS
Venetian, XVII Century
Rectangular marbleized column, enriched with scrollings and leafage carved in high relief; surmounted by a voluted capital.
Height, 43 inches.

332. OAK CRICKET TABLE
Jacobean Period
Circular top; triangular underframing, on three polygonal legs.
Height, 27 inches; diameter, 26½ inches.

333. SILK NEEDLEPOINT WALNUT ARMCHAIR
Charles II Period
Oblong canted back, and seat covered in fine needlework exhibiting on a black ground in soft tones of rose, variegated greens and reds, conventionalized foliations; scrolled and voluted acanthus-carved arms projecting beyond spiraled supports. On spiraled and block stretchered legs.

334. INLAID WALNUT LOWBOY
Queen Anne Period
Oblong hinged top, which, with the frieze, opens to compartmented interior; the front fitted with three small drawers; arched valance having a trifid pendant; on cabriole legs and slipper feet.
Height, 31 inches; width, 28 inches.

335. WALNUT CHEST-OF-DRAWERS
Jacobean Period
In two sections. Oblong overhanging top; fitted with one drawer having raised vertical panels, flanked by split balusters; the lower section with three drawers similarly flanked. Trimmed with hexagonal brasses with drop loop handles. On bun feet.
Height, 39 inches; width, 39 inches.

59

336. SET OF SEVEN HEPPLEWHITE MAHOGANY CHAIRS
                                    English, XVIII Century
Comprising six side chairs and one armchair. Shield-shaped open back, with pierced vase splat; "stretched up" leather seat; on tapered square legs with spade feet.

337. CARVED WALNUT COFFRET   *French Renaissance*
Rectangular hinged top; the sides beautifully carved in the Renaissance manner, exhibiting Vitruvian scrolls composed of dolphins. wyverns and grotesque masks. On molded base. (Back and base restored.)
                    Height, 13½ inches; length, 26 inches.

338. INLAID WALNUT CHEST-OF-DRAWERS   *Queen Anne Period*
Oblong cyma-molded top; the front fitted with two end-on drawers and three graduated drawers, trimmed with cinquefoil brasses with drop handles. On bracket feet.
                    Height, 35½ inches; length, 39 inches.

339. CHIPPENDALE MAHOGANY CONSOLE TABLE
                                    English, XVIII Century
Triangular folding top opening to a square, having lunetted corners; on four cabriole legs with shell-carved knees; pad feet. One adjustable leg. The surface has been refinished at a later date.
                    Height, 27½ inches; length, 36 inches.
        Note: This table can either be used as a centre table or a side table.

340. SHERATON MAHOGANY DINING TABLE   *English, XVIII Century*
Oblong top, with two folding flaps, reeded at the edges and having rounded corners; on vase-baluster and curule-shaped supports, brass bound at the toes.
        Height, 2 feet 4 inches; width, 4 feet 1½ inches; length extended, 5 feet 2 inches.

341. SHERATON MAHOGANY DINING TABLE   *English, XVIII Century*
Similar to the preceding.

342. CHIPPENDALE MAHOGANY CENTRE TABLE
                                    English, XVIII Century
Oblong top with two folding flaps and having leaf-carved edges: the underframing fitted with a drawer at either side. On tapered square legs.
                    Height, 28 inches; length, 42 inches.

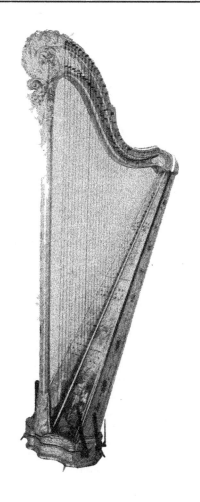

343. DECORATED LAQUÉ HARP   *By Erard, XVIII Century*

/ C. Beautifully painted, depicting a garden scene with court ladies and a courtier before a background of feathery leafage. The scrolled top finely carved and gilded; the angular body *semé* with sprays of forget-me-nots.

Height, 5 feet 2½ inches; width, 2 feet 4 inches.

344. CARVED MAHOGANY CARD TABLE   *English, XVIII Century*

Folding top, with semicircular outset and dished corners, the under-framing with a succession of cyma-curves centring a shell motif. On cabriole legs with leaf- and shell-carved knees; molded pad feet. One gated leg.

Height, 28½ inches; length extended, 33 inches.

345. INLAID MAHOGANY SIDE TABLE   *English, XVIII Century*

Oblong molded top with line of zig-zag inlay; the front fitted with one shallow drawer flanked by two square drawers, enriched with oval brasses and bail handles. Two spandrels of the kneehole are bracketed with fretted scrolls. On square tapered legs.

Height, 31 inches; length, 33½ inches.

346. OAK BUREAU   *Jacobean Period*

Rectangular molded top, with dentil cornice molding; the front fitted with long frieze drawer simulating two drawers, and double doors with raised panels of geometrical motifs flanked by split balusters and enclosing nest of three drawers. On block feet.

Height, 34 inches; length, 38½ inches.

347. CARVED WALNUT ARMCHAIR   *Charles II Period*

Oblong open back, with spirally twisted uprights and leaf-carved finials; the top rail carved with reticulated and voluted leafage centring a putto; slightly splayed scrolled and voluted arms; seat and back *cannés;* on spirally twisted and block stretchered legs. The design of the top rail is repeated in the frontal stretcher.

348. FOUR CARVED WALNUT SIDE CHAIRS   *Charles II Period*

Open canted back, with spirally twisted uprights with ball finials; the top rail carved with scrolled leafage centring a shell motif, the vertical panels a rosette; seat and back *cannés;* on spirally twisted stretchered legs.

349. ELM WINDSOR ARMCHAIR   *English, XVIII Century*

Comb-back, with pierced vase-shaped splat; molded arms on baluster supports; saddle seat; on turned stretchered legs.

350. RARE YEW WINDSOR ARMCHAIR   *English, XVIII Century*

Comb-back, with pierced vase-shaped splat flanked by four spindles; balustered uprights supporting outcurving flat arms; saddle-seat, on turned outspreading legs connected by H-stretcher.

351. CARVED MAHOGANY TRIPOD TABLE *Chippendale* Period
Serpentined square top chamfered at the corners, with echinus molded edges; on fluted and quilled columnar shaft and tripod support with shell-carved knees and leaf-carved pad feet.

Height, 32 inches; width, 16 inches.

352. CHIPPENDALE CARVED MAHOGANY DROP-LEAF BREAKFAST TABLE
English, XVIII Century
Molded oval top; on four carved cabriole legs terminating in ball feet.

Length, 59 inches; width, 52 inches.

353. ADAM MAHOGANY CONSOLE TABLE *English, XVIII* Century
Rectangular top, banded with mahogany of a differing grain; the underframing and four rectangular tapering legs finely canalated; the knee blocks enriched with oval paterae.

Height, 33½ inches; length, 51½ inches.

354. CRIMSON DAMASK WALNUT WING CHAIR *Queen Anne* Period
Serpentined broad back and wings and lunette-shaped seat, covered in fine floral damask; supported on bracketed cabriole legs with shell-carved knees and pad feet.

355. CHIPPENDALE CARVED MAHOGANY THREE-TIER DUMBWAITER
Tripod base with leaf-carved feet, supporting three graduated shelves with carved molded borders divided by urn-shaped and carved columns.

Height, 42 inches.

356. TWO CHIPPENDALE CARVED MAHOGANY BOOKSHELVES
English, XVIII Century
Fretted sides, carved in an interlaced Chinese pattern, tapering at top and base and supporting four shaped shelves.

Height, 38 inches; length, 18 inches.

357. INLAID WALNUT CHEST-OF-DRAWERS ON STAND
Queen Anne Period
In two sections. Oblong cove- and cyma-molded top; the upper section with two small and three long drawers, the stand with one small drawer above the arched valance flanked by two larger drawers; on bracket feet. Trimmed with bat's-wing brasses and bail handles.

Height, 50 inches; width, 39 inches.

63

358. Pair Carved Walnut Side Chairs   *Charles II Period*

—Oblong open back, slightly spooned and raked, having spiraled uprights, with urn finials, enclosing a *canné* panel flanked by voluted leafage and crested by a winged cherub head centred by foliage: *canné* seat: on curious S-scrolled front legs. With frontal stretcher of recurring design.

359. WALNUT MARQUETERIE CHEST-OF-DRAWERS

William and Mary Period

Oblong molded top; the front fitted with two small and three long drawers, enriched with horizontal arched panels of laburnum having curved ends exhibiting in fine marqueterie a floral design; trimmed with original pear-drop handles, on bun feet.

Height, 36½ inches; length, 37 inches.

65

360. WALNUT TREASURE CHEST   *Northern Italian, XV Century*

Massive rectangular overhanging top; the front and sides enriched with original wrought iron mountings, consisting of hasp and lock, handles and reticulated circular dies mounted upon crimson velvet. On mediaeval carved lion supports. When opened the top reveals interesting *intarsia* inlay.

Height, 25 inches; length, 47 inches.

Note: A companion chest *is* i*ll*ustrated in Schottmüller's *Furniture of the Italian Renaissance*, page XXII, and *is* in the Schloss Museum at Berlin.

(Illustrated)

361. CRIMSON CUT VELVET WALNUT ARMCHAIR   *Italian Renaissance*

Open back, with a slight rake, and leaf-carved finials; unusually broad molded flat arms. Ring and knopped turned stretchered legs; the frontal stretcher finely carved and exhibiting in relief a winged sphinx flanked by scrolled foliage. Seat and back in contemporary crimson cut velvet on an ivory ground, and trimmed with scalloped fringe.

362. NEEDLEPOINT WALNUT WING CHAIR   *Queen Anne Period*

l c c. Serpentined back, wings, outscrolling arms and seat covered in brilliantly colored needlework displaying a conventionalized floral motif, on bracketed cabriole legs with shell-carved knees and slipper feet.

(*Illustrated*)

363. TWO CARVED WALNUT SIDE CHAIRS   *James II Period*

High slightly raked back with inset central upholstered panel, flanked by vertical slender balusters and surmounted by a fine arched cresting of voluted and scrolled foliage. The seat tapering to the rear, is supported on scrolled Flemish legs braced by an H-stretcher and having a frontal stretcher exhibiting baroque influence. Covered in old-blue velvet.

364. TWO CARVED WALNUT SIDE CHAIRS   *James II Period*

Similar to the preceding.

365. TWO CARVED WALNUT SIDE CHAIRS   *James II Period*

Similar to the preceding.

366. OAK JOINT STOOL   *Jacobean Period*

Rectangular molded top; molded box frieze; on splayed columnar box stretchered legs.

Height, 22 inches; width, 16½ inches.

367. SPANISH WALNUT SIDE TABLE   *XVII Century*

Rectangular massive overhanging top; the frieze drawer paneled to a lozenge motif and having cyma-curved valance. On reel-turned box stretchered legs and bun feet.

Height, 29 inches; length, 33 inches.

368. CARVED WALNUT SIDE TABLE   *Spanish, XVIII Century*

Oblong overhanging top; the frieze fitted with two drawers having knop handles and cyma-curved valance, and carved to a latticed and lozenge motif: on reel-turned box stretchered legs, developing the same motif.

Height, 30½ inches; length, 34½ inches.

369. OVAL MAHOGANY EXTENSION DINING-TABLE

English, XVIII Century

Beautifully grained mahogany top, reeded at the edge; with box frieze; on six round tapered reeded legs. Five extension leaves; the extending device is a Victorian addition and ingeniously arranged.

Height, 29 inches; length, 54 inches.

370. WALNUT SIDE TABRLE   *Spanish, XVII Century*

Rectangular overhanging top; the frieze fitted with two end-on drawers exhibiting a cartouche motif. On turned box stretchered columnar legs.

Height, 28 inches; length, 33½ inches.

371. CARVED OAK CHEST   *Jacobean Period*

Oblong molded top; the front paneled and fitted as double enclosing doors; finely carved with scrolled and voluted strap-work, alternating with rosettes. On quadrangular supports. Fine patina.

Height, 24½ inches; length, 41½ inches.

372. WALNUT MARQUETERIE KNEEHOLE WRITING-DESK

William and Mary Period

425

Oblong top, with ovolo cornice molding; the front fitted with one long drawer, a recessed central cupboard door, flanked at either side by three small drawers, supported on bun feet. The whole structure enriched with superb arabesque or seaweed marqueterie and veneer of ebony.

Height, 32½ inches; length, 40 inches.

69

373. WALNUT BENCH   *William and Mary Period*

Rectangular *canné* seat; supported by eight gadrooned octagonal legs, braced by gracefully curved stretchers set saltirewise, with molded terminals. Loose cushion covered in amethyst velvet, paneled in broad gold galloon.

Height, 1 foot 2½ inches; length, 5 feet 7 inches.

(*Illustrated*)

374. RENAISSANCE TAPESTRY WALNUT ARM CHAIR

Oblong high back and seat, covered in fine sixteenth century Flemish tapestry, developing at the back a rustic scene: centring the composition is a seated maiden with a sheaf of corn; the seat exhibiting fruit and foliage. Beautifully scrolled arms, legs and open stretcher in the Carolean manner.

375. RENAISSANCE NEEDLEPOINT WALNUT SETTEE   *Carolean Style*

Rectangular back; outscrolling arms and loose seat cushion covered in rare Renaissance needlepoint. The back panel depicting a mediaeval citadel, in the foreground knightly warriors are taking leave of their womenfolk, and receiving blessings. The seat cushion with conventionalized motifs. The frame of later date with turned and block legs braced by hooped frontal stretchers in the Carolean manner.

Height, 3 feet 1 inch; length, 6 feet 6 inches.

376. RARE CARVED OAK GATE-LEG TABLE   *Tudor Period*

Oval top having two rule-jointed leaves: the frieze fitted with one deeply molded drawer having drop loop handle: supported by four bulbous gadrooned legs braced by a nulled box stretcher. Two of the legs are split and hinged to form gates.

Height, 29 inches; length extended, 54 inches.

No. 373. WALNUT BENCH
(*William and Mary Period*)

71

377. Needlepoint Carved Mahogany Pole Screen

Chippendale Period

Oblong *torsade* molded frame enclosing panel of old English needlepoint, exhibiting a jardinière of flowers within an arcaded setting hung with grape-vines. On tripod support finely carved, with claw-and-ball feet.

Height, 52 inches; width, 23 inches.

72

378. SET OF EIGHT INLAID MAHOGANY LADDER-BACK CHAIRS

Chippendale Period

Comprising six side chairs and two armchairs. Open square back, having four horizontal pierced bars in ladder form, the crowning rail inlaid with a scrolled and voluted oak-leaf emitting a chain of pendent husks; approximately square slip seat in crimson damask, the seat rail exhibiting flat-carved oval patera; on quadrangular H-stretchered legs, inlaid at the front to simulate channeling.

73

379. CARVED WOOD EAGLE CONSOLE TABLE
English, XVIII Century

Realistically carved screeching eagle with wings displayed, perched upon a rocaille structure, with Bavarian marble top. Fine patina.

Height, 30½ inches; length, 50½ inches.

380. GROS AND PETIT POINT MAHOGANY WING CHAIR
English, XVIII Century

Serpentined back and wings with outscrolling arms and square seat covered in fine needlepoint, the back depicting stag hounds attacking and about to close with a stag, the seat and arms in richly colored foliations. On rectangular stretchered legs.

381. WALNUT SIDE TABLE　　　　*Spanish, XVII Century*

Massive overhanging top; the frieze fitted with one drawer paneled with four cruciform motifs. On reel-turned, box stretchered legs.

Height, 29 inches; length, 30 inches.

382. WALNUT SIDE TABLE　　　　*Spanish, XVII Century*

Similar to the preceding, with slight variation in drawer.

Height, 27½ inches; length, 31 inches.

383. NEEDLEPOINT WALNUT WING CHAIR　*English, XVIII Century*

Oblong serpentined back and wings with scrolled arms and loose seat cushion, covered in fine needlepoint depicting in brilliant colors of greens, blues, reds and fawns on an ivory ground bold design of fruit and flowers. On cabriole legs.

384. HEPPLEWHITE CARVED MAHOGANY BANQUETTE
English, XVIII Century

Serpentined seat, with outscrolling arm-rests; the seat rail finely gadrooned; supported on carved slightly cabriole legs with feet resembling a dolphin's head. Covered in a blue material.

Height, 26 inches; length, 49 inches.

385. HEPPLEWHITE CARVED MAHOGANY BANQUETTE
English, XVIII Century

Similar to the preceding.

386. CARVED OAK BREAD CUPBOARD ON STAND　　*Jacobean Period*

In two sections. Rectangular molded top; the front fitted with double enclosing doors, having spindled grille, the stiles and rails incised and carved to a laureled and strap motif. Lower section frieze arcaded and fluted, resting on columnar box stretchered legs.

Height, 50 inches; width, 33½ inches.

74

387. SHERATON INLAID KINGWOOD OCCASIONAL COMMODE

English, XVIII Century

900. Of curvilinear contour, in the French taste. Serpentined oblong top; the slightly swelling fall-front, disclosing three small drawers, is flanked by ormolu mounts of chains of pendent husks which continue as a banding to the incurving tapering legs and terminate in cabochon and cartouched toes. The top and sides, inlaid with hollywood and sycamore, exhibit within entwined scrollings a trellis and quatrefoil motif. *Height, 28 inches; width, 19½ inches.*

388. BLACK AND GOLD LACQUERED CHEST-ON-STAND

English, XVIII Century

450. Rectangular hinged top, which with the sides is beautifully lacquered and exhibits a minute lozenge design, upon which is superimposed a grapevine leafage and tendril motif in slightly raised gold. The stand with four tapered square legs similarly enriched.

Height, 44 inches; width, 40½ inches.

Note: This chest was probably lacquered by an Oriental in England.

(*Illustrated*)

75

389. CARVED MAHOGANY PEDESTAL WRITING TABLE

English, XVIII Century

In three sections. Oblong top with tooled leather inset: leaf-carved edges: fitted with six drawers, three at either side: resting on end pedestals opening as cupboards: at the reverse end with drawers. Trimmed with original brasses with ring handles.

Height, 30 inches; length, 60 inches.

390. MADONNA AND CHILD   *By Nathan Drake, British,* 1750-1783

Half-length seated figure, in profile to left, wearing crimson and blue mantle, holding a sleeping lightly draped child upon her knee, a veil covering the heads of both figures.

Height, 30 inches; width, 24 inches.

Signed on back of canvas, N. DRAKE. PINXT, and dated 1776.

391. DECORATIVE OIL PAINTING

Attributed to Sir William Beechey, English, 1753-1807

LADY MARY ANN PIGOT. Three-quarter length life size figure, facing the observer, seated by a window and before a draped crimson curtain; wearing a simple white dress, and holding an open letter in her right hand.

Height, 50 inches; width, 40 inches.

392. DECORATIVE OIL PAINTING

Attributed to Angelica Kauffmann, English, 1753-1839

AURORA AND TITHONUS. Charming depiction, in soft colors, of the legend of "Aurora and Tithonus." Tithonus, having received the honor of immortality, is conveyed by a chariot drawn by prancing white steeds and attended by a cupidon and celestial maidens to the presence of Aurora, the goddess of Dawn, the beautiful winged figure seen to the right.

Height, 3 feet 2 inches; length, 8 feet 2 inches.

393. TWO PAINTED OVERDOORS   *French School, XVIII Century*

(A) Charming depiction of sporting putti reveling in a corn field: at the left, two small semi-draped figures, one carrying a sheaf of corn, the other a sickle; at the right a sleeping putto being crowned with wheat-ears by his companion. (B) Depicting four semi-draped putti, one kneeling by a freshly kindled fire: at the right a small figure being draped by his companion. In carved and parcel-gilded frames.

Height, 26 inches; length, 42 inches.

76

394. DECORATIVE OIL PAINTING
School of Jean Marc Nattier, French, 1685-1766

60. —Three-quarter length figure of a court lady, facing the observer, wearing loose flowing robes of gold with a blue sash.

Height, 39 inches; width, 32 inches.

395. TWO OIL PAINTINGS *Italian School, XVIII Century*

Displaying with classic feeling picturesque ruins at the edge of a *130.* —bay. The scenes animated by various figures in bright costumes.

Height, 32 inches; length, 41½ inches.

396. OIL PAINTING *School of Charles Van Loo, French, 1705-1765*

FISHERMEN. In the foreground a seated court lady and a courtier *250.* —with a small Charles spaniel, before a background of foliage; at the right four fishermen hauling in their net; in the middle distance a bridge with further figures of fishermen.

Height, 38 inches; length, 59 inches.

397. SET OF OLD ENGLISH NEEDLEWORK STATE BED HANGINGS
XVII Century

2200. —Comprising two side curtains, one bedspread, one back curtain and five valances. Depicting an adaptation of the *chou-fleur* design superbly colored and worked in pinks, blues, reds, browns and fawns appliqué on a fine Chinese blue satin ground.

Two side curtains: Height, 7 feet 7 inches; width, 3 feet 11 inches.
Bedspread: Height, 7 feet 5 inches; length, 8 feet 2 inches.
Back curtain: Height, 7 feet 5 inches; length, 8 feet 2 inches.
Three valances: Length, 5 feet; depth, 1 foot 5 inches.
Two valances: Length, 6 feet 1 inch; depth, 1 foot 5 inch.

398. VERDURE TAPESTRY *Aubusson, XVII Century*

CASTLES IN LANDSCAPE. Richly wooded undulating scene depicting *95.* — in the middle distance a picturesque château before which is a lake with two idling swans. In the foreground a bridge spans the lake and flanking the arches are two sea lions; at the right lambs are grazing, and at left a parrot. Woven in shaded greens, browns, tans and blues.

Height, 7 feet 11 inches; length, 12 feet 4 inches.

77

399. BRUSSELS TAPESTRY   *XVIII Century*

SANCHO PANZA AND DAPPLE. Don Quixote's squire is seen standing
about the centre foreground of rising country, his ass Dapple is
toward right under a clump of trees and near a flowering bush; at
left beyond a small pool is a hound before some brambles; in mid-
distance is a stream flanked by two groups of trees and flowing
before a large château. Woven in rich greens, blues, crimsons, tans,
yellows, grays and fine warm ivories. Exceptionally interesting border executed in richer colors than the field, on deep Havana-brown
grounds, exhibiting trailing clusters of fruit interrupted by dogs,
birdcages with songsters; and at upper left and right-hand corners
are birds' nests with fledglings being fed by their parents.

Height, 8 feet 11 inches; width, 6 feet 3 inches.

(*Illustrated*)

400. VERDURE TAPESTRY   *Aubusson, XVIII Century*

LANDSCAPE WITH BIRDS. Richly wooded landscape with a vista of
a spired château with a dove volplaning towards it, and a pathway
leading through the middle distance. To the right of the château
is a spiraled column. In the right foreground a heron, while on
either side are rich woodlands in full foliage. Woven in shaded
browns, blues, greens, and ivory.

Height, 8 feet; length, 8 feet 5 inches.

401. IMPORTANT CARVED WALNUT CREDENZA

Florentine Renaissance

Rectangular molded top with floriated lunette-carved edges, the
front fitted with two frieze drawers, and double enclosing doors,
flanked by pilaster blocks carved in relief with cherubim masks,
and pilasters with caryatid figures. The drawers finely carved with
winged cherubim figures, the doors paneled with a lozenge motif.
On bun feet.

Height, 37½ inches; length, 49 inches.

No. 399. BRUSSELS TAPESTRY
(*XVIII Century*)

79

402. IMPORTANT CARVED OAK COURT CUPBOARD   *Jacobean Period*
Oblong molded soffited top, with deeply nulled cornice: the frieze
enriched with a conventionalized foliated lozenge motif. on pillar-
turned supports: the recessed top having a sunk and nulled central
panel flanked by two cupboard doors exhibiting archaically portrayed birds amidst leafage. The lower section with lunette-carved
frieze. three deeply recessed panels similarly carved, beneath which
are two carved and paneled doors. The whole structure with finely
molded stiles on turned supports.

Height, 6 feet; width, 4 feet 10 inches.

From the Collection of the Late Sir John Milbanke, Bart., Norton
Manor, Radnorshire, England.

(Illustrated)

403. CARVED OAK WAINSCOT CHAIR   *Cromwellian Period*
High oblong paneled back, carved with a lozenge enclosing a guilloche and a quatrefoil motif; open scrolled arms. on baluster supports which continue as legs connected by a box stretcher; the seat
rail enriched with foliated lunettes.

404. IMPORTANT CARVED OAK COURT CUPBOARD   *Carolean Period*
Quaintly pendented oblong overhanging frieze, enriched with interlacing floriated lunettes and inscribed: D A R · 112 · 1676:
recessed front with two enclosing doors having lozenge motifs and
incised roundels. flanked by arcaded panels adorned with palmated
strap-work and conventionalized leafage: the lower section enclosed
by two doors with well-proportioned panels and original wrought
iron hinges: the fillet-molded stiles continue as quadrangular
supports.

Height, 5 feet; length, 6 feet 5½ inches.

Note: This cupboard is of unusual length.

405. CHINOISERIE OVER-MANTEL MIRROR   *French, XVIII Century*
Oblong beveled mirror, flanked by latticed mirrors; above is a
decorative oil painting of an Eastern scene, enclosed by a frame
of bamboo stems in leafage. At the four corners are salamanders.

Height, 5 feet 1 inches; length, 6 feet.

No. 402. IMPORTANT CARVED OAK COURT CUPBOARD
(*Jacobean Period*)

81

406. SEVEN CHINOISERIE MURAL PAINTINGS *French, XVIII Century*
Landscape scenes depicted in fine color in the Chinese manner, por-
traying figures at various pursuits. The rich gold-embroidered
Eastern costumes especially being executed with great brilliance.

*Height, 9 feet; widths, 6 feet 3 inches, 7 feet 2 inches, 6 feet 8 inches; 3 feet 1
inch: 6 feet 3 inches: 7 feet 2 inches, and 6 feet 3 inches.*

(*One illustrated*)

407. SHERATON INLAID SATINWOOD KNEEHOLE WRITING-DESK
English, XVIII Century
Oblong top, with tooled leather inset; the front fitted with one long
drawer and six small drawers and a recessed central cupboard door;
trimmed with bail handles; on bracket feet.

Height, 30 inches; length, 31 inches.

408. TWO ADAM CARVED AND GILDED PEDESTALS
English, XVIII Century
In graceful tripod form with three slender shafts; claw feet, and
cornucopia-like tops emitting three winged sphinxes adorsed, surmounted by a circular disk; the convex base enriched by anthemion
motives centred by a vase finial.

Height, 66 inches.

409. INLAID WALNUT SLANT FRONT SECRETARY BOOKCASE
Queen Anne Period
In two sections. Rectangular cove and cyma-molded top: double
enclosing doors having shaped mirrors: the slant front opening to
fitted interior. The lower section fitted with two small and two
long drawers: on bracket feet. Trimmed with original brasses and
bail handles.

Height, 6 feet 9 inches: width, 3 feet 3½ inches.

410. CARVED MAHOGANY PIE-CRUST TABLE *Chippendale Period*
Tilting slightly sunk circular top, with molded pie-crust edge: supported on vase baluster shaft and tripod support having eagle
claw-and-ball feet. The tripod finely carved at the knees.

Height, 28 inches; diameter, 30½ inches.

No. 406. Seven Chinoiserie Mural Paintings
(*French, XVIII Century*)

83

Kindly read the Conditions under which every item is offered and sold. They are printed in the forepart of the Catalogue.

411. NEEDLEPOINT CARVED MAHOGANY ARM CHAIR
Chippendale Period

Broad square back, seat, and arm-rests covered in superb needle-point, the back depicting within a cartouched frame a court lady, the seat a conventionalized floral motif. The downcurving quadrangular supports and legs finely carved with strap-work containing leafage and quatrefoils.

412. KINGWOOD AND TULIPWOOD COMMODE MOUNTED IN CUIVRE DORÉ
Louis Quinze Period

The serpentined *bombé* front fitted with two drawers, exhibiting an attractive lozenge motif centring quatrefoils, which is continued to the sides; on incurving graceful legs. The original rocaille ormolu mountings finely chased. Siena marble top.

Height, 33½ inches; length, 38½ inches.

413. TWO SHERATON MAHOGANY PEDESTALS WITH URNS
English, XVIII Century

Rectangular, with hinged doors paneled with applied moldings and lines of a lighter color inlay; on bracket feet. Classic urns, the lower periphery carved with acanthus leafage.

*Height of pedestals, 41 inches; width, 22 inches.
Height of urns, 31 inches.*

The following set of walnut and tooled leather armchairs, numbers 414-419, are from the Collection of the Duke of Northumberland, Stanwich Hall.

414. TWO WALNUT AND TOOLED LEATHER ARMCHAIRS
Italian Renaissance

Tall open back, with gilded leaf finials and panel of finely tooled leather enriched with armorial bearings; flat molded arms projecting beyond baluster supports; rectangular leather covered seat with deep valance and fringe; on quadrangular side stretchered legs, with embryonic claw feet.

415. TWO WALNUT AND TOOLED LEATHER ARMCHAIRS
Italian Renaissance

Similar to the preceding.

416. TWO WALNUT AND TOOLED LEATHER ARMCHAIRS
Italian Renaissance

Similar to the preceding.

417. TWO WALNUT AND TOOLED LEATHER ARMCHAIRS
Italian Renaissance

Similar to the preceding.

(*Illustrated*)

418. TWO WALNUT AND TOOLED LEATHER ARMCHAIRS
Italian Renaissance

Similar to the preceding.

419. TWO WALNUT AND TOOLED LEATHER ARMCHAIRS
Italian Renaissance

Similar to the preceding.

85

No. 422. Carved and Gilded Pine Wood Wall Garniture
(*George I Period*)

86

420. LOUIS XIV NEEDLEWORK AND UPHOLSTERED SOFA

Oblong back, slightly flaring scrolled arms and three loose cushions. Covered in attractive *Louis Quatorze* needlepoint and depicting in fine colors on an *écru* ground a bold foliated motif in variegated blues, greens and reds.

Height, 2 feet 10 inches; length, 6 feet 3 inches.

421. CARVED OAK REFECTORY TABLE   *William and Mary Period*

Massive rectangular top, the underframing finely carved with an interesting strap motif alternating with cabochons, supported by six ringed pillar turned bulbous members with block feet, stoutly braced by a rounded box stretcher.

Height, 2 feet 7 inches; length, 9 feet 2 inches.

422. CARVED AND GILDED PINE WOOD WALL GARNITURE

George I Period

Comprising: (A) Mirror of architectural contour; the entablature carved in bas-relief with sporting putti, surmounted by an interrupted pediment centred in an urn finial; supported by Corinthian capitaled columns which enclose Greek meander bordered mirror. (B) Four wall carvings, depicting a large convex shell framed in acanthus leafage and enclosing classic male and female masks upon which are superimposed displayed eagles perched on laurel wreaths; at the base are leonic masks from which depend swags. (C) Two wall carvings, portraying classic profile masks adorsed, from which depends a cartouche enclosing a sunflower; above are two-handled vases emitting foliage. . In original gilding.

Mirror: Height, 8 feet 4 inches; width, 4 feet 9½ inches.
Four carvings: Height, 8 feet 2 inches; width, 2 feet 8½ inches.
Two carvings: Height, 8 feet 4½ inches; width, 1 foot 9½ inches.

(*Illustrated*)

423. PAIR WROUGHT IRON GATES   *Florentine, XVI Century*

Vertical bars, having at the ends mascarons within a heart-shaped device and winged cherubim heads; the horizontal panels with graceful scrollings and tendrils; crested by a scroll and lanceolate motif; lion mask and drop loop handles.

Height, 7 feet 11 inches; width, 5 feet ¾ inch.

→►{END OF SECOND SESSION}◄←

THIRD AND LAST SESSION

FRIDAY, MAY 7, AT 2:15 P. M.

Catalogue Numbers 424 to 603 Inclusive

424. SILK BROCADE PHOTOGRAPH FRAME

Rectangular frame, covered in fine old rose-crimson floral brocade.

Height, 15 inches; width, 12 inches.

425. ROSE-CRIMSON DAMASK PHOTOGRAPH FRAME

Rectangular cyma-molded frame, covered in fine old damask and banded with gold galloon.

Height, 15 inches; width, 12 inches

426. ROSE-CRIMSON DAMASK PHOTOGRAPH FRAME

Rectangular cyma-molded frame, covered in fine old damask and banded with gold galloon.

Height, 15 inches; width, 12 inches.

427. CELADON VASE   *Ming*

Deep bowl-shape, with expanding lip: engraved under the glaze with dragons and other motifs. (Rim chipped.)

Height, 6 inches.

428. VICENZAN OVAL BRONZE PLAQUETTE

By Valerio Belli, 1465-1546

Modeled in low relief, depicting OUR LORD BEARING THE CROSS ON THE ROAD TO GOLGOTHA, harassed by mounted Roman centurions and soldiery. Signed, VALERIUS VICENTIUS. F. Other examples of Belli are in the *Louvre* and one is in the Berlin Museum illustrated in its catalogue, plate LXIV.

Height, 3½ inches; length, 3¾ inches.

From the Stefano Bardini Collection, American Art Association, 1918.

429. BRONZE INKSTAND   *Italian, XVI Century*

Circular bowl with domed cover, having finial composed of a winged cherub clutching a goose: the sides enriched with mascarons: on three rudimentary claw feet. The cover of a later period, the finial of the sixteenth century.

Height, 4¾ inches.

89

430. BRONZE INKSTAND   *Venetian, First Half XVI Century*
Circular bowl. supported by three seated putti adorsed; with flat-
molded cover. having classic warrior figure as finial.

Height, 7 inches.

431. GEORGIAN SILVER INKSTAND
Rectangular pierced and compartmented frame. displaying graceful
scrollings and gadrooning. On scrolled leaf supports. Cut glass
fittings. London hall mark, 1766-7.

Height, 7½ inches.

432. BRONZE STATUETTE   *Italian, Early XVII Century*
HERMES. Erect well-modeled figure. with closely curled hair and
wings; carrying in his right hand the caduceus. On circular marble base.

Height of statuette, 8 inches

433. FRAMED WAX PORTRAIT   *English, XVIII Century*
Bust-length: finely modeled figure of the Empress Catherine of
Russia. In an oval gilded frame.

Height, 8 inches.

434. BRONZE INKSTAND   *Italian, XVI Century*
Kneeling figure of Atlas. supporting a leaf-molded cauldron-shaped
bowl with dome cover: on elongated octagonal base. The bowl
and base are later additions.

Height, 10 inches.

435. SILVER CANDELABRUM   *French, XVIII Century*
Vase baluster stem. emitting two scrolled arms with urn-shaped
bobéches for lights; on hexagonal splayed base. Fitted with an
oval adjustable yellow silk shade.

Height, 15½ inches.

436. BLUE SILK BROCADE PHOTOGRAPH FRAME
Rectangular frame. covered in fine old peacock-blue and gold
brocade.

Height, 15 inches; width, 12¼ inches.

437. BLUE SILK BROCADE PHOTOGRAPH FRAME
Rectangular frame. covered in fine old peacock-blue and gold
brocade.

Height, 15 inches; width, 12¼ inches.

438. PAIR POLYCHROME ENAMEL CANDLESTICKS

Limoges, XVII Century

Baluster stem, on splayed and octagonal base. Depicting within oval medallions a coat of arms. and three bust-length classic figures inscribed: Adonis. Cephale. Lavrore.

Height, 6 inches.

439. PAIR CELADON ANIMAL STATUETTES *Ch'ien-lung*

Figure of the sacred duck. on rock base; in dense celadon glaze. (One wing restored.)

Height, 7½ inches.

440. PAIR SMALL CELADON VASES MOUNTED IN CUIVRE DORÉ

K'ang-hsi

Club-shaped: in fine luminous green. depicting in powder-blue. trees. cloud scrollings and animalistic figures tinged with *rouge de fer;* circular ormolu base.

Height, 11 inches.

From the Collection of the Countess of Essex.

441. CRIMSON VELVET BOUDOIR DESK SET

Comprising oblong box. desk tray. blotter and book-ends. Banded in gold galloon; the box and book-ends enriched with embroidered medallions.

442. NEEDLEWORK SILK DAMASK PHOTOGRAPH FRAME

Rectangular frame. covered in fine old English needlework and peacock-blue Spitalfields silk damask.

Height, 15¼ inches; width, 12¾ inches.

443. NEEDLEWORK SILK DAMASK PHOTOGRAPH FRAME

Rectangular frame, covered in rare old English needlework and peacock-blue Spitalfields silk damask.

Height, 15¼ inches; width, 12½ inches.

444. GOLDEN-YELLOW DAMASK PHOTOGRAPH FRAME

Rectangular frame. covered in fine damask: the front trimmed with *bleu de ciel* damask edged with gold and green silk narrow galloon.

Height, 15¼ inches; width, 12 inches.

91

445. AMETHYST VELVET AND NEEDLEPAINTED BOUDOIR SET

Comprising rectangular photograph frame, desk box and folding
blotter. Covered in rare Renaissance velvet and banded with gold
galloon.

446. LARGE NEEDLEPOINT PHOTOGRAPH FRAME

Oblong ogival arched frame, covered in old English needlepoint
depicting on an *écru* ground a series of quatrefoils in shaded blues
and other motifs in moss-green. Banded with old-rose guimpe.

Height, 19½ inches; width, 16 inches.

447. GOLD-EMBROIDERED CRIMSON VELVET CUSHION

Italian Renaissance

Oblong; the central panel beautifully wrought in gold and silken
threads, depicting within an oval panel, THE VISITATION OF SAINT
ANNE, enclosed within a rich gold border. The back in crimson
damask. Trimmed with crimson and gold fringe.

448. NEEDLEPOINT CUSHION   *English, XVIII Century*

Square; the central medallion, depicting, in the Chinese manner, a
pagoda flanked by cypress trees, on an ivory ground.

449. NEEDLEPOINT CUSHION   *English, XVIII Century*

Square; depicting within a scrolled cartouche beneath a pagoda
Eastern figures in the Chinese manner. Trimmed with ball fringe.

450. ROSE-CRIMSON CUT VELVET PHOTOGRAPH FRAME

Rectangular cyma-molded frame, covered in fine old velvet and
banded with gold galloon. The back in crimson damask.

Height, 15½ inches; width, 12½ inches.

451. AUBERGINE VELVET PHOTOGRAPH FRAME

Rectangular molded frame, covered in fine old velvet and banded
with silver galloon. Back and interior in moss-green brocatelle.

Height, 12¾ inches; width, 10½ inches.

452. CELADON-GREEN VELVET PHOTOGRAPH FRAME

Rectangular cyma-molded frame, covered in fine old velvet. Back
in *vieux rose* velvet. Banded with silver galloon.

Height, 15½ inches; width, 12½ inches.

453. GOLD-EMBROIDERED AND BROCATELLE CUSHION
Italian Renaissance

Square; the centre with panel depicting in fine needlepoint a saintly figure within an arched canopy. Trimmed with golden-yellow fringe.

454. GOLD-EMBROIDERED AND BRO-CATELLE CUSHION
Italian Renaissance

Square; the central panel in fine needlepoint, depicting St. Agnes, banded with gold galloon. Trimmed with fringe.

(*Illustrated*)

455. NEEDLEPOINT CUSHION *English, First Half of XVIII Century*

Square; depicting the quartered shield of the Earls of Cadogan, the corner spandrels in *gros point*. Trimmed with variegated green ball fringe.

456. RENAISSANCE NEEDLEPAINTED AND CRIMSON VELVET STATIONERY CASKET

Rectangular, with p o i n t e d arched top; portraying in superb needlepoint the figure of St. Paul; at the back an escutcheon. On short square legs.

Note: Very rare.

(*Illustrated*)

93

457. RENAISSANCE NEEDLEPAINTED AND CRIMSON VELVET FOLDING
BLOTTER

Serpentined arched top; portraying in fine needlepoint within an
arched niche St. Anthony of Padua.

Note: Very rare.

(Illustrated)

458. TAPESTRY CUSHION   *Flemish Renaissance*

Square; depicting within a central floral medallion, The Last Sup-
per, with Our Lord surrounded by His Apostles, a star forming
the nimbus. Beautifully woven in fine colors of variegated blues,
browns, rose-crimson, golden-yellows and greens. With peach-
toned silk back. Trimmed with blue fringe.

459. TAPESTRY CUSHION   *Flemish Renaissance*

Square; portraying within a circular floral medallion The Cruci-
fixion, in which appear the proverbial figures. Superbly woven in
fine colors of greens, reds, tans and golden-yellows on an *écru*
ground. The back in peach-toned silk. Trimmed with blue fringe.

460. TAPESTRY CUSHION   *Flemish Renaissance*
    Square; depicting, within a circular floral medallion, The Nativity. In fine blues, rose-crimson, golden-browns and variegated greens. The back in peach-toned silk. Trimmed with blue fringe.

461. BEADWORK CASKET   *Charles II Period*
    Oblong hinged top, richly decorated and depicting a male and female figure, trees, a lion and leopard; the sides with vinery, flowers, a mounted figure and other personages: in greens, white, yellows and blues on an ivory-satin ground.

Height, 7 inches; length, 13 inches.

462. POWDER-BLUE ROSE BOWL   *K'ang-hsi*
    Beautifully glazed and depicting in gold, various *chinoiserie* landscape scenes.

Diameter, 7½ inches.

463. LARGE FAMILLE ROSE BOWL   *Ch'ien-lung*
    Circular; richly decorated and paneled by scrollings depicting two animated *chinoiserie* scenes. In the finely glazed colors of the *famille-rose*. On carved teakwood stand.

Height, 6½ inches; diameter, 15½ inches.

464. TURQUOISE-BLUE BEAKER   *Sung*
    Finely glazed and decorated in relief with leafage, birds and trophies.

Height, 8 inches.

465. TWO VERY FINE WORCESTER SCALE BLUE VASES
    Decorated with shaped oval medallions representing long tailed birds with very bright plumage: marked with a rare square mark of the Worcester factory.

Height, 8 inches.

466. TWO FAENZA EWERS   *Italian, XVI Century*
    Globular, with tapering neck and circular foot: loop strap handle and straight short spout, supported by a loop; richly decorated in fine turquoise-blue, cobalt, green, red and golden-yellow. Inscribed upon the central banding: Ossi 2 Acara and Si² · D · Acoro. (Slight reparations.)

Height, 10½ inches.

467. PAIR FAENZA MAJOLICA EWERS   *Renaissance Period*

Oviform, with strap handle and upturned short spout. Inscribed within cartouches: Mel Rosat Zv and Svdepomis. Enameled in fine blues, greens and golden-brown on a white ground.

Height, 9½ inches.

468. GEORGIAN REPOUSSÉ SILVER EPERGNE

Graceful motif of a fruiting vine; reticulated domed base on pastoral supports, superimposed by a fruit basket with two small figures of the infant Bacchus: four boughs branch from the base as supports for sweetmeat cut glass dishes. London hall mark, 1766-7.

Height, 13½ inches; length, 16½ inches.

469. RARE INLAID AND CARVED BONE JEWEL CASKET
    French, XIV Century

Hexagonal, domed top, enriched with horizontal panels exhibiting flying angels and interesting *intarsia* inlay: the sides having eighteen small plaquettes depicting mediaeval figures carved in bas-relief; hexagonal base with serrated edge.

Height, 8¼ inches.

470. PAIR BOTTLE-FORM VASES MOUNTED IN CUIVRE DORÉ *Ch'ien-lung*

In the Ming manner. Globular with tall neck and tulip form lip: having on the body two saurians molded in relief; of fine blue-gray glaze with an all pervading crackle; on Louis Quinze ormolu base.

Height, 13½ inches.

471. BLACK BASALTES BUST   *Wedgwood-Etruria, XVIII Century*

HORACE. Finely modeled head of the poet facing the observer; on circular base.

Height, 14½ inches.

472. PAIR CUIVRE DORÉ CANDELABRA   *Louis Seize Period*

Putto seated upon a dolphin bearing an urn upon his shoulder emitting two branches with lily-form *bobèche;* on circular marble base.

Height, 13½ inches.

473. RARE CELADON VASE   *Sung*

Elliptical, with incurving neck and base; coated with a uniform glaze of smooth brilliance over a boldly incised diaper patterning; broad crackle.

Height, 8 inches.

See Frank's "Oriental Porcelain," Folio 6.

474. FAMILLE ROSE ET NOIRE JARDINIÈRE MOUNTED IN CUIVRE DORÉ
Ch'ien-lung

160. — Broad and low cylindrical form; on a black ground are gorgeously colored chrysanthemums and sprays of leafage.

Diameter, 9 inches.

475. IMPORTANT LARGE FAMILLE VERTE VASE *K'ang-hsi*

Club-shaped; with long cylindrical neck and flanged lip; depicting in
200. — the fine colors of the *famille verte* the state visit of a mandarin with attendant personages. (Repaired.)

Height, 29½ inches.

476. CHINESE LOWESTOFT DINNER SERVICE *XVIII Century*

Comprising: Forty-one dinner plates, eighteen soup plates, sixteen graduated platters, five fruit dishes of various sizes, twelve cake
1100. — plates, ten sweetmeat dishes, four gravy bowls, four small covered tureens with trays and two very large covered tureens. Beautifully glazed translucent porcelain decorated on a creamy-white ground enriched with floral sprays and scrollings in deep old-rose. (Slight imperfections.)

477. DECORATED PORCELAIN DINNER SERVICE
Spode, XVIII Century

75. — Comprising: Eighty dinner plates, fifteen soup plates, fifteen platters, twelve fruit dishes (four square, four boat-shape and four shell-shape), twenty cake plates, eleven sweetmeat dishes, four covered tureens and one compotier. Similar to and matching the preceding dinner service and made by the Spode factory.

478. BLUE AND WHITE DINNER SERVICE *Spode, XVIII Century*

Comprising: Five dinner plates, two small covered tureens with trays, two small trays, large covered soup tureen with tray and ladle, three covered and two uncovered vegetable dishes, salad dish, sauce-boat, fourteen graduated platters and four knife rests. On a finely glazed white ground displaying in cobalt-blue old English landscape scenes.

479. URBINO MAJOLICA BOWL *Italian Renaissance*

Circular, with scalloped rim and fluted sides on splayed foot. Decorated in the Raphaelesque manner and in the characteristic colors of Urbino. The embossed *tondino* exhibiting a bathing figure.

Diameter, 13½ inches.

97

480. HISPANO-MORESQUE LUSTRE PLAQUE   *XVI Century*

C.   —Deep cavetto, enriched with the lion rampant in fine cobalt; amidst
scrollings and conventionalized floral motifs; deep golden lustre.

Diameter, 16½ inches.

(*Illustrated*)

481. MOSS-GREEN CELADON BOWL   *Ming*

Shallow bowl, with incurving neck and flaring lip, having embryonic
handles of grotesque masks and three stump feet. Brilliant celadon
glaze. (Repaired.)

Diameter, 11½ inches.

482. RARE FAIENCE GROUP   *By Bernard Palissy, French, XVI Century*

CHRIST AND THE WOMAN OF SAMARIA. At the left is the seated
figure of Our Lord resting by the well, wearing an aubergine mantle; at the right is the standing figure of the woman come to draw
water similarly glazed in aubergine and wearing a green head-
dress. (One hand missing.)

Height, 6½ inches.

98

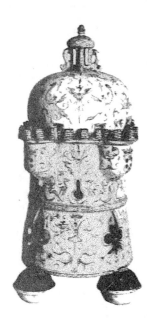

483. RARE URBINO MAJOLICA TOWER   *XVI Century*

In two sections. Circular crenelated tower of Veneto-Byzantine
contour with battlements. loopholes and domed roof superimposed
by a further domed small observation tower. On four bulbous supports. Richly decorated in the Raphaelesque manner of Urbino
with harpies. grotesques, cupidons. cornucopiae and the Medici
arms.

Note: Very unusual specimen.   *Height, 16¼ inches.*

(*Illustrated*)

484. FAIENCE MAJOLICA EWER   *French, XVI Century*

Depressed spherical body. with knopped spout and scrolled cartouche; arched bail handle upon which is a seated dog. Splayed
circular foot. Richly enameled in fine blues. golden-browns and
greens and decorated in the Renaissance manner. (Repaired.)

Height, 14 inches.

485. STATUARY MARBLE AND CUIVRE DORÉ MANTEL CLOCK
By Folin à Paris

Circular dial, surmounted by two doves flanked by rams'-masks; supported on a marble column flanked by sphinxes. Rectangular base.

Height, 13 inches; width, 9 inches.

486. CARVED WALNUT COFFRET   *Italian Renaissance*

Sarcophagus-shape: finely molded hinged top; the front and sides gadroon-paneled; the front with a central escutcheon flanked by angels emitting Vetruvian scrollings. The deeply molded base with reversed foliated lunettes; on paw feet.

Height, 13 inches; length, 21 inches.

487. STUART NEEDLEWORK AND STUMP-WORK CASKET

Rectangular top, depicting in fine needlework and stump-work a garden with male and female figures: each side with small panels representing figures and animals: executed in bright colors on white silk ground.

Length, 12 inches; width, 10 inches; height, 7 inches.

488. BISQUE AND ORMOLU MANTEL CLOCK   *By Bergmiller à Paris*

Circular white dial in an octagonal setting, surmounted by a classically draped figure seated upon a Wedgwood blue pedestal, flanked by urns of flowers. Oblong base enriched with a gilded bronze plaque.

Height, 16 inches; width, 10 inches

489. PAIR BRONZE STATUETTES   *Italian, XVII Century*

(A) DAVID. Erect youthful figure. his foot on the head of Goliath; classically draped, and wearing winged petasus, his sword reversed in his left hand, his right raised. On verte antique marble base.
(B) ARES. Erect galeated figure. wearing classic armor and bearing a shield on the left arm and a javelin in his right. On verte antique marble base.

Height of statuettes, 18 inches and 18½ inches.

490. SET OF THREE SHERATON MAHOGANY KNIFE BOXES
English, XVIII Century

Slant-front, of beautifully grained mahogany, having original silver claw-and-ball feet and mounts. The largest box with original fittings, the two smaller ones have been adapted for stationery.

Heights, 18 and 14 inches; widths, 12¼ and 9½ inches.

491. CHINESE CHIPPENDALE CARVED AND GILDED WALL MIRROR

English, XVIII Century

Oblong mirror: the cresting centred by a curiously perched flamingo, before a scrolled arcading: the sides similarly carved and enriched with bunches of grapes, leafage and stalactite motifs: the base having within reversed C-scrolls two concave cockle-shells.

Height, 5 feet 8 inches: width, 3 feet 10 inches.

492. CHINESE CHIPPENDALE CARVED AND GILDED MIRROR

English, XVIII Century

Irregular oblong mirror enclosed within a beautifully carved frame, having an interrupted scrolled pediment centring a mandarin seated beneath a pagoda: at the shoulders are male and female busts carved in full relief, beneath are other *chinoiserie* motifs, flamingoes and stalactite ornamentation. Very fine mirror with original gilding.

Height, 6 feet 9 inches; width, 4 feet.

493. CARVED WALNUT SIDE TABLE *Spanish Renaissance*

Oblong top: the frieze drawer enriched with cruciform motifs and knop handle: reel-turned box stretchered legs.

Height, 27½ inches: length, 29½ inches.

494. MAHOGANY AND ROSEWOOD DWARF SECRETARY

English, XVIII Century

Oblong top: the slant-front opening to interior fitted with drawers and pigeon-holes: beneath are four cock-beaded drawers trimmed with original bail handles. On bracket feet.

Height, 37 inches; width, 23½ inches.

495. TWO JACOBEAN WALNUT ARMCHAIRS *English, XVII Century*

Low back, the seat and back covered in green striped velvet, the back having in the centre a lion rampant holding a sword and a cup, worked in metal threads: spirally twisted arms; on four similar legs connected by H-stretchers.

496. WALNUT SIDE TABLE *William and Mary Period*

Oblong molded top: the box frieze fitted with single drawer: on spirally twisted legs braced by a curiously curved stretcher set saltirewise. On bun feet.

Height, 29 inches; length, 32 inches.

497. DECORATIVE OIL PAINTING

> *In the manner of François Boucher, French, 1703-1770*
> PORTRAIT OF A LADY. Before a background of a terraced garden,
> an erect stately figure standing by a garden urn, wearing rose-crimson gown of the period and holding a floral wreath in her left
> hand: the powdered hair coiffed high and braided over her shoulder.

Height, 25 inches; width, 21 inches.

498. OIL PAINTING   *By Giovanni Paolo Pannini, Italian, 1695-1768*

> RUINS. At the left the ruins of a classic Corinthian palace, on the
> steps of which are itinerant musicians, dancers and wine sellers; at
> the right in the foreground, an obelisk; beyond in the harbor an
> anchored warship and a turreted castle with a bowman's tower is
> seen to the right.

Height, 28½ inches; length, 48½ inches.

499. OIL PAINTING   *By Giovanni Paolo Pannini, Italian, 1695-1768*

> RUINS. At the edge of a bay, the scene animated by peasants, is
> the ruined façade of a Corinthian palace, under a vaporous blue
> sky flecked with gray clouds.

Height, 28½ inches; length, 48½ inches.

500. CARVED OAK BENCH   *Jacobean Period*

> Rectangular molded top, enriched with flat-carved border of conventional scrolled leafage; molded underframing, on four splayed
> columnar legs with block feet.

Height, 22½ inches; length, 59½ inches.

Note: The "flat-carved" border is of the period, and very unusual.

501. TWO GEORGIAN CARVED MAHOGANY REVOLVING ARM CHAIRS
    English, XVIII Century

> Shaped back with scrolled top, carved with a leaf motif in relief;
> circular seat; on four square fluted legs.

502. OAK JOINT STOOL   *Jacobean Period*

> Rectangular molded top and underframing; on columnar box stretchered legs with block feet which have an outward spread.

Height, 21½ inches; width, 18 inches.

503. CARVED OAK WAINSCOT CHAIR   *Cromwellian Period*

> Arched panel back with cresting of foliated lunettes and central
> quatrefoil carved in relief, enriched with conventionalized tulips;
> down-curving arms and molded square seat, the seat rail with recurring lunette motif, on vase baluster and block stretchered legs.

504. CARVED OAK CONSOLE TABLE   *Régence Period*

Oblong: the frieze beautifully carved and reticulated with leafage and enriched with floral motifs in relief: supported by reversed scroll legs embellished with festoons of flowers and rocaille motifs, connected by X-stretcher with shell terminal. *Brèche violette* marble top.

Height, 31 inches: length, 56 inches.

505. QUEEN ANNE MARQUETERIE AND WALNUT GRANDSIRE CLOCK
By John Hamers, London, XVIII Century

Tall case, fitted with one door inlaid with floral marqueterie: the front of the base with a panel inlaid with similar motifs: the hood enclosed by a glazed panel door, flanked by two columns similarly inlaid; ormolu, dial and steel centre engraved with Roman numerals: second hand, pierced hour and minute hands.

Height, 7 feet 6 inches.

506. INLAID WALNUT SECRETARY-BUREAU   *Queen Anne Period*

Oblong top; the slant-front opening to interior fitted with two small drawers, numerous pigeonholes and central cupboard flanked by *bonheur-du-jour* compartments: the front fitted with two small and two long drawers having chased bat's-wing brasses and bail handles. On bracket feet.

Height, 36½ inches; width, 29½ inches.

507. SMALL INLAID WALNUT SECRETARY-BUREAU

Queen Anne Period

Oblong top: the fall-front, which rests upon a tray, opening to fitted interior: beneath are four drawers banded and cross-banded with mahogany and trimmed with bat's-wing brasses and bail handles. On block supports.

Height, 36½ inches; width, 27½ inches.

508. OAK CRICKET TABLE   *Jacobean Period*

Circular top: triangular slightly arched underframing; on three polygonal legs.

Height, 28 inches; diameter, 27 inches.

509. SET OF FIVE DAMASK WALNUT ARMCHAIRS   *Cromwellian Period*

Oblong back and seat covered in deep *drap d'or* crimson damask, exhibiting a Renaissance design. The straight arms and legs with the characteristic knop turning.

103

510. CARVED MAHOGANY PEDESTAL STRIKING CLOCK
By Frodsham of London, circa 1810

Circular dial enclosed within a lyre-shaped case, reeded and carved with foliage, surmounted by a gadrooned dome with classic urn finial; the base similarly carved and supported on rosetted bracket feet.

Height, 36¼ inches; width, 19½ inches.

Note: Exceptional chiming movement, no less than six melodies can be played at the hours.

(*Illustrated*)

511. CARVED OAK WAINSCOT CHAIR   *Jacobean Period*

Back paneled in two sections, the square panel flat-carved with lozenge motif, the horizontal panel with floriated lunettes, surmounted by a leaf-carved cresting. Downcurving voluted arms and paneled seat. On columnar box stretchered legs.

512. CHIPPENDALE CARVED MAHOGANY CARD TABLE
English, XVIII Century
Hinged folding and lifting top, having leaf-carved edges and outset lunetted and dished corners, the underframing molded to the same contour. On leaf-carved cabriole legs with pad feet. Two legs are gated to support leaf.

Height, 28 inches; length, 32 inches.

513. SET OF THREE CARVED WHITE MAHOGANY ARMCHAIRS
Chippendale Period
Cartouche- shaped back and seat, finely carved in a restrained and pleasing vein, exhibiting delicate rocaille motifs; the padded arms longitudinally curved and voluted, on S-scrolled uprights; supported by reversed C-scrolled voluted legs, on leaf toes. Covered in crimson damask.

Note: Extremely rare and interesting specimens in the French taste. The design of these chairs appears in the original publication of Chippendale's *Cabinetmaker and Director.*

514. OAK MARQUETERIE CHEST *Jacobean Period*
Oblong molded hinged top; the front having within double arches supported by canalated pilasters, fine panels of floral marqueterie flanked by split balusters. On block supports.

Height, 27 inches; length, 49½ inches.

515. INLAID ROSEWOOD OCCASIONAL TABLE
English, XVIII Century
Serpentined top with drop-leaves, banded and cross-banded with various fruitwoods and exhibiting a meander leaf motif; graceful shaped underframing; supported by four slightly cabriole legs, the toes enriched with *cuivre doré* mounting.

Height, 30 inches; length, 37½ inches.

516. CARVED WALNUT ARMCHAIR *Charles II Period*
Open canted back, with spirally twisted uprights and small vase finials; the cresting between the uprights characteristic of an early period with deeply molded scrolls centring the rose; open scrolled and voluted arms projecting beyond spiral supports; *cannés* back and seat, on spirally twisted stretchered legs. With crimson velvet loose cushion.

517. CARVED OAK FOOD CUPBOARD   *Cromwellian Period*

Arcaded superstructure with central knopped pendant; the stiles and rails gouged to a guilloche motif; the lower section paneled, exhibiting a palmated chain patterning; central cupboard door pierced and balustraded. (The bun feet have recently been added by Mr. Dawson.) *Circa* 1645.

Height, 38½ inches; width, 29½ inches.

Note: Illustrated in *"The Dictionary of English Furniture,"* by Percy Macquoid and Ralph Edwards, Vol. II, page 204, Fig. 6.

518. IMPORTANT NEEDLEPOINT CARVED MAHOGANY ARMCHAIR
Chippendale Period

Broad square seat and back covered in superb needlepoint, depicting in brilliant colors a mythical scene enclosed within a cartouche and animalistic figures. Downcurving arms join rosetted curule supports; on cabriole legs with lion-claw feet and carved knees.

From the Collection of the Earl of Strathmore, Streatham Castle, County Durham.

519. IMPORTANT NEEDLEPOINT CARVED MAHOGANY ARMCHAIR
Chippendale Period

Similar to the preceding; with slight variation in needlework.

From the Collection of the Earl of Strathmore, Streatham Castle, County Durham.

520. TWO CRIMSON BROCATELLE WALNUT STOOLS
William and Mary Period

Square seat; in fine crimson cut velvet, trimmed with fringe; on octagonal trumpet legs and bun feet, braced by interestingly scrolled stretchers set saltirewise and centred by a bossed roundel.

Height, 18 inches; (top) 16 inches square.

521. TWO CRIMSON BROCATELLE WALNUT STOOLS
William and Mary Period

Similar to the preceding.

Height, 18 inches; (top) 16 inches square.

522. THREE MARQUETERIE WALNUT SIDE CHAIRS
William and Mary Period

Open back, with arched cresting which is an extension of the vase-shaped splat, and, with the voluted upright, is inlaid with fine floral marqueterie; cyma-curved seat rail with central device carved with shell motifs; leaf-carved cabriole legs with pad feet connected by H-stretcher. Slip seat in *drap d'or* cut crimson velvet.

Note: Very fine chairs of this epoch showing Dutch influence.

523. PAIR ADAM CARVED AND GILDED TORCHÈRES
English, XVIII Century

Circular top, supporting classic urn-shape vase emitting two branches with *cuivre doré bobèches* for lights; on three graceful incurving supports having at the top rams'-masks connected by chains of beads and terminating in rams' hoofs.

Height, 5 feet 10 inches.

107

---

524. HEPPLEWHITE MAHOGANY ARMCHAIR *English, XVIII Century*
Oval back and serpentined seat, covered in fine French green floral
brocade; the frame of delicate proportions with outcurving short
arms and graceful incurving supports; on slightly cabriole legs terminating in a scroll resembling a dolphin's head.

525. OAK CENTRE TABLE *Jacobean Period*
Rectangular molded top, supported on four vase balustered legs
braced by a molded box stretcher.
Height, 30 inches; length, 53 inches.

526. GROS AND PETIT POINT MAHOGANY FIRE SCREEN
Queen Anne Period
Arched oblong frame on splayed supports, enclosing needlepainted
subject, THE JUDGMENT OF SOLOMON, portrayed with interesting
perspective in an architectural setting. In fine greens, fawns,
browns, blues and reds.
Height, 58 inches; width, 27½ inches.

527. IMPORTANT CARVED WALNUT REFECTORY TABLE
Italian Renaissance
Oblong molded massive top, supported by solid lyre-shape end sup-
ports, braced by a central transverse centring a bossed roundel,
securely mortised and tenoned.
Height, 2 feet 9 inches; length, 8 feet 4 inches.
Note: A very fine table.

528. PRIMITIVE OIL PAINTING *Northern France, Late XV Century*
VOTIVE ALTAR PANEL. Depicting three scenes from the life of
Christ. From left to right: THE NATIVITY, THE ADORATION OF
THE MAGI, and THE BAPTISM OF OUR LORD BY JOHN THE BAPTIST.
The work portrayed with characteristic charm and a perfection of
color which is the very quintessence of French art of the Quat-
trocento.
Panel: Height, 2 feet; length, 6 feet 6 inches.
Note: The ancient French inscription describes the panel as a donation to a hospital.

(*Illustrated*)

108

No. 528. PRIMITIVE OIL PAINTING
(*Northern French, Late XV Century*)

109

529. ADAM CARVED AND GILDED OVAL MIRROR

English, XVIII Century

Oval mirror, enclosed by fluted and leaf-carved frame; at the shoulders are profile rams'-masks emitting chains of pendent husks. Knotted bow ribbon cresting centring a honeysuckle motif; at the base graceful vase enriched by an oval patera and scrolled and voluted leafage.

Height, 6 feet 7 inches; width, 4 feet 2 inches.

From the Collection of Lord Louth, Louth Hall, Ardee, County Louth.

530. ADAM CARVED AND GILDED OVAL MIRROR

English, XVIII Century

Similar to the preceding.

Height, 6 feet 7 inches; width, 4 feet 2 inches.

From the Collection of Lord Louth, Louth Hall, Ardee, County Louth.

531. HEPPLEWHITE MAHOGANY LOVE SEAT *English, XVIII Century*
Of curvilinear contour; closed arched back and outcurving arms, the frames fillet-molded, fluted and quilled; on four turned and reeded short tapering legs. Covered in eighteenth century floral jade-green damask.

Height, 35½ inches; length, 37½ inches.

532. HEPPLEWHITE MAHOGANY LOVE SEAT *English, XVIII Century*
Similar to the preceding.

Height, 35½ inches; length, 37½ inches.

533. FINE NEEDLEPAINTED PANEL *Queen Anne Period*
Interesting composition portrayed in harmonious colors in *petit point;* a distant view of mediaeval castles amid undulating wooded landscape. In the foreground within a balustraded ground, two classic athletes are engaged in a ball game; at the right within a raised canopied enclosure, an Emperor is seated with his Empress intent upon the game; leaning by the balustrade are attendant galeated figures, while at the right a trumpeter sounds a fanfare. Border of Renaissance tapestry.

Height, 35 inches; width, 27 inches.

110

534. NEEDLEPOINT PANEL   *Charles II Period*

A crouching tiger and a prancing stag are seen in the midst of a
bold floral design, around are various birds. Broad floriated border. In finely shaded tones of blues, reds, greens, fawns and
browns.

Height, 40½ inches: length, 60 inches.

III

535. FINE CRIMSON VELVET AND GOLD APPLIQUÉ BANNER
Italian Renaissance

Rich crimson field bordered by a scrolled Renaissance design enclosing a cartouche finely wrought in gold thread, in which is depicted
Saint Nicholas of Myra with his emblems. Fish-tail ends; with
deep gold fringe.

Height, 47½ inches; width, 29 inches.

(*Illustrated*)

536. FINE CRIMSON VELVET AND GOLD APPLIQUÉ BANNER
Italian Renaissance

Similar to the preceding but depicting Saint James.

(*Illustrated*)

537. SET OF RARE CREWELWORK STATE BED HANGINGS
Jacobean Period

Comprising bedspread, back curtain, two side curtains and valances.
Depicting on an écru ground boldly scrolled foliage and figures of
a stag and a tiger in browns shading to golden-yellows and variegated greens.

Two side curtains: Height, 6 feet 9 inches; width, 2 feet 10 inches.
Two large curtains: Height, 7 feet 6 inches; width, 5 feet 5 inches.
Long valance: Length, 21 feet 4 inches; depth, 15 inches.
Short valance: Length, 8 feet; depth, 10 inches.

Note: Extremely rare, and could be adapted as three pairs of curtains with valances.

538. SET OF RARE CREWELWORK STATE BED HANGINGS
Jacobean Period

Bold foliated design characteristic of this old English crewelwork
depicted on an écru linen field with brilliantly colored birds and
other animals in shaded greens and rose shading to red and browns.

Bedspread: Length, 6 feet 11 inches; width, 7 feet 6 inches.
Back curtain: Length, 7 feet 11 inches; width, 6 feet 6 inches.
Two side curtains: Length, 7 feet 6 inches; width, 2 feet 10 inches.
Two valances: Length, 6 feet 8 inches; width, 1 foot 6 inches.

Note: Extremely rare and could be adapted as three pairs of curtains with valances.

535   536

Nos. 535 and 536. FINE CRIMSON VELVET AND GOLD APPLIQUÉ
BANNERS
(*Italian Renaissance*)

539. DELFT RENAISSANCE TAPESTRY

Karel van Mander, Artist and Weaver, 1548-1623

An historical event from the Court of François I enacted within the mythical garden of the Temple of Apollo. Executed with great artistry, interesting perspective, and fine rendering of lighted and shaded textures. In the right foreground is the regal figure of the King with his consort, and the remorseful Dauphin (later Henri II) regarding his deposed mistress Diane de Poitiers; at the left. with her head inclined towards the mitred Bishop, is the statuesque Catherine de Medici with her train bearer in the wake of the advancing figures of Anne de Montmorency and Constable Montmorency. The classic formal garden is flanked by arcaded avenues with the Temple of Renaissance contour to the right, and the fountain of Venus in the middle distance, around which are grouped various court ladies and nobles, in gorgeous raiment. In the background, which possesses great depth, is the labyrinth of Ariadne, the colossus silhouetted against the peaked landscape; deer are watering at the lake. The monogram KVM appears upon the shield with a lion as supporter, surmounting the fluted column at the left. Finely woven in harmonious shades of reds, blues, greens, golden-yellows, fawns and browns.

Height, 8 feet 2 inches; length, 14 feet 2 inches.

Note: Karel van Mander was formerly pattern-painter to the Spierincx manufactory at Delft, but rivaled his master, and was commissioned by King Christian IV of Denmark to weave the now famous tapestries at Castle Frederiksborg; he was also responsible for the famous Venetian Room set at Knole Park, which much resembles this tapestry.

(Illustrated)

No. 539. DELFT RENAISSANCE TAPESTRY
(*By Karel van Mander, Artist and Weaver, 1548–1623*)

540. GARDEN TAPESTRY *Louis Quinze, First Half of XVIII Century*

A formal terraced garden with fountains playing at either end; at the right the balustraded façade of an elegant château of fine architectural proportions, somewhat obscured by the trees in full leafage, and before which are arranged with care classic garden urns with dwarfed trees; in the middle distance the dower house faintly silhouetted. In the foreground, rich with shrubbery and delineated with a subtle sense of values, are a gorgeous peacock and his hen perched beneath a fruiting tree. Woven in charming fawns shading to browns, blues, greens and reds.

Height, 7 feet 10 inches; length, 15 feet 3 inches.

(*Illustrated*)

No. 540. GARDEN TAPESTRY
(*Louis Quinze, First Half of XVIII Century*)

541. FLEMISH RENAISSANCE TAPESTRY   *XVI Century*

THE CHASE (*Fantasia*). Interesting portrayal of a fabulous scene, executed with a rigorous attention to minute detail, and with a perfection of technique. In the richly wooded forest pandemonium reigns among the animals, before the advance of the regal figures astride prancing horses, with attendants afoot; in the foreground a stupendous bull is charging a leopard, an ape is climbing a tree, a heron and a wild boar, and to the right a stag seemingly terror-stricken. Through the forest setting, a distant château and domestic buildings are vigorously depicted. The original borders are enriched with jardinières and fruit motifs, harpies, masks, and satyrs; at the lower left and right corners are differing depictions of Diana. The tapestry is finely woven in greens, blues, reds and golden-yellows.

Height, 10 feet; length, 15 feet 6 inches.

(*Illustrated*)

No. 541. FLEMISH RENAISSANCE TAPESTRY

(XVI Century)

542. FLEMISH RENAISSANCE TAPESTRY *XVI Century*

THE CHASE (*Fantasia*). Before a background of wooded lands, richly preserved, with spired châteaux, an animated hunting party is advancing, with attendant beaters. In the foreground a ferocious griffin is in deadly combat with a coiled reptile, while to the right is a startled fallow deer and a fluttering pelican; at the left by the stump of a tree a prancing horse, a lizard, and a stag making for the more thickly wooded forest. The unusually fine border displays fruit, flowers and foliage arranged with great charm, at the lower right and left corners are erect figures, an armed warrior and a maid beneath canopies. Beautifully woven in harmonious soft tones of fine madder reds, shading to browns, fawns, greens and blues.

Height, 10 feet 3 inches; length, 16 feet 4 inches.

(*Illustrated*)

No. 542. FLEMISH RENAISSANCE TAPESTRY
(XVI Century)

543. FLEMISH RENAISSANCE TAPESTRY   *First Half XVI Century*
PERGOLA TAPESTRY. Beautiful specimen of weaving, portraying a
symbolism of husbandry, viewed through a triple arched pergola
supported by canephore and decked with fruit and foliage; cresting the central arch are reclining classical figures, flanking them are
winged angels and pastoral figures, and below a unicorn, the emblem
of chastity and a huge fabulous bird probably denoting avarice;
about this charmingly arranged scene are various other animals
of the forest in curious attitudes, racing hither and thither through
the wood. Seated upon the balustrading are youthful figures with
musical instruments. Superbly woven in blues and greens, tawny-
tans, browns and ivory, and possessing the original narrow meander
border.

Height, 10 feet 9 inches; length, 14 feet 8 inches.

Note: An excellent example of the tapestry technique of this epoch.

(*Illustrated*)

No. 543. FLEMISH RENAISSANCE TAPESTRY
(*First Half XVI Century*)

123

544. GOTHIC TAPESTRY   *English, XV Century*

CEADWALLA OF WALES. The warlike King, arrayed in armour, and seated astride a powerful prancing gray charger, held by an attendant man-at-arms, is brandishing a spiked bludgeon, probably at the court jester to the left. On the trappings of the charger is blazoned the DRAGON OF WALES; on the trunk of the massive tree to the right, an escutcheon bears the arms of Ceadwalla. The background is occupied by a many turreted and bastioned mediaeval castle, and the foreground by a millefleurs patterning, and a small bear. Interestingly woven in finely shaded tones of reds, blues, greens, browns and fawns.

Height, 9 feet 1 inch; width, 8 feet 7 inches.

Note: This rare tapestry is probably of Barcheston weave.

(*Illustrated*)

No. 544. Gothic Tapestry
(*English, XV Century*)

125

545. BRUSSELS TAPESTRY   *Flemish Renaissance*

MOSES DELIVERING THE PEOPLE OF ISRAEL. The depiction is at
the decisive moment when the hosts of Pharaoh are engulfed by
the raging sea, through which the Israelites have passed with safety.
The central figure of the composition is that of Moses slightly to
the right with other figures arrayed behind him, one in an attitude
of reverential fear. In the foreground at the left a female and a
male figure are resting, while others hurry forward to those by the
encampment, already offering thanks by sacrifice for their deliver-
ance. The superb original border enriched by cartouched medallions flanked by bucrania, fruiting and flowering motifs. Woven in
finely shaded colors of reds, blues, greens, and golden-browns.

Height, 11 feet 4 inches; length, 17 feet 8 inches.

(*Illustrated*)

No. 545 Brussels Tapestry
(Flemish Renaissance)

127

546. HEPPLEWHITE CARVED MAHOGANY CABINET-SECRETARY
English, XVIII Century

Oblong molded top; the front interestingly fitted with two reticulated and beautifully traceried doors, composed of scrolled leafage and tulips and six drawers, also a central panel which pulls down and is supported by quadrants, revealing interior fitted for writing, with twelve small drawers faced with amboyna-wood, and pigeonholes. On quadrangular tapering legs with spade feet. Trimmed with fretted brasses and ring handles.

Height, 5 feet 1 inch; width, 3 feet 1 inch.

547. IMPORTANT ADAM CARVED MAHOGANY BOOKCASE
English, XVIII Century

In two sections of architectural contour. Slightly outset centre with a segmental hood. The frieze, astragal-fluted, interrupted by oval paterae, is supported by voluted modillions from which depend chains of foliage and flowers carved in relief, enclosing three gracefully traceried glazed doors. The lower section of similar contour, is fitted with three doors beautifully paneled with crotched mabogany, flanked by half columns and pilasters of Doric form fluted and quilled. Above the doors are oval paterae and suspended encarpa motifs.

Height, 7 feet 7½ inches; width, 5 feet 8 inches.

From the collection of Lord Carden, Templemore, Co. Tipperary.

(*Illustrated*)

No. 547. HEPPLEWHITE CARVED MAHOGANY CABINET-SECRETARY
(*English, XVIII Century*)

548. TWO ADAM CARVED AND GILDED OVAL MIRRORS

English, XVIII Century

550. Oval mirror, enclosed by an astragal and leaf-carved frame; having at the shoulders the profile rams'-masks characteristic of the Adelphi; suspended from an oval patera by chains of oak-leaves in pressed vellum; at the base is further foliage in the same media.

Height, 49½ inches; width, 23 inches.

From the Collection of Lord Louth, Louth Hall, Ardee, Co. Louth.

(One illustrated)

130

549. CARVED PINE CONSOLE TABLE

By William Kent, English, circa 1730

Oblong top, with leaf carved cyma-molding and fluted frieze. centring a satyr mask and emitting festoons of oak leaves; supported on four quadrangular incurving legs carved with leafage and cinquefoils terminating in claw feet. Brocatelle marble top.

Height, 34 *inches; length,* 41½ *inches.*

(*Illustrated*)

550. PAIR BRONZE ALTAR CANDLESTICKS   *Italian, XVII Century*

Finely modeled vase-balustered and knopped stem, enriched with cherubim heads, winged angels and other Renaissance motifs. supported by a scrolled and voluted trilateral base terminating in lionclaw feet, which is further embellished with angels, masks, and cartouched escutcheons. Fitted for electricity. Domed shade with heavy silk fringe.

Height, 6 *feet* 10 *inches.*

Note: Modeled in the manner of Sansovino and having a rich Renaissance patina.

551. PAIR GILDED BRONZE AND ROCK CRYSTAL CANDELABRA
George I Period

Trilateral and cartouched baluster stem, emitting three scrolled branches with *bobêches* for candles, from which depend large pear-shaped rock crystal drops. On triangular incurving base enriched with three figures of harpies.

Height, 22½ inches.

(*Illustrated*)

552. PAIR ADAM CARVED AND GILDED PEDESTALS
English, XVIII Century

Tripod form, composed of quadrangular incurving columns, terminating in *pieds de biches* and having acanthus capitals which support a triangular palmated and laureled volute terminating in rams'-heads. Central vase motif on incurving plinth.

Height, 57 inches.

(*Illustrated*)

553. IMPORTANT CRIMSON VELVET CARVED IRON-WOOD STATE CHAIR
Flemish, XVI Century

Rectangular back and seat covered in Renaissance crimson velvet; the back having finials composed of Brabant lions bearing an escutcheon; voluted, scrolled and leaf-carved arms with curious leonic masks projecting beyond vase-baluster supports; on slender legs connected by double box stretcher, one notched, the other cymacurved; on knopped feet.

554. SHERATON INLAID MAHOGANY SIDEBOARD
English, XVIII Century

Shaped front, fitted with long drawer flanked by two cupboards; the fronts simulating drawers, trimmed with original brass handles; above is a shelf fitted with one long drawer and two side drawers; supported by six square tapering legs inlaid with floral motifs.

Length, 6 feet 3 inches; height, 44 inches.

No. 551. Pair Gilded Bronze and Rock Crystal Candelabra
(*George I Period*)

No. 552. Pair Adam Carved and Gilded Pedestals
(*English, XVIII Century*)

133

555. IMPORTANT CARVED MAHOGANY SETTEE   *George I Period*

Beautifully carved double hoop backs of fine proportions, with solid lyre-shape splats carved with acanthus leafage and crested with cockle shell motifs.   Longitudinally curved and voluted arms; oblong "stitched-up" seat covered in fine foliated needlepoint; on cabriole legs with shell-carved knees and claw-and-ball feet.

Height, 42 inches; length, 60 inches.

Note: This settee and the following chairs form a unique set.

(*Illustrated*)

556. SET OF FIVE CARVED MAHOGANY SIDE CHAIRS

George I Period

Similar to the preceding settee, with slight variation in the needle-point on two chairs.

(*Illustrated*)

557. TWO RENAISSANCE TAPESTRY WALNUT ARMCHAIRS

Serpentined oblong back and seat in fine sixteenth century *Flem*-
O. ish tapestry, illustrating within cartouches on an *écru* ground. epi-
sodes from "Aesop's *Fables*," jardinières of flowers, fruit and verdure. *Longitudinally* curved and voluted arms; turned and block
stretchered legs, with arched frontal stretcher. *Frames* in the *Louis*
Treize manner.

558. Two Renaissance Tapestry Walnut Armchairs
Louis XIII Style

Similar to the preceding.

559. Two Renaissance Tapestry Walnut Armchairs
Louis XIII Style

Similar to the preceding.

560. Two Chinese Chippendale Carved and Gilded Girandoles
English, XVIII Century

Scrolled cartouche-shaped, of rocaille and stalactite motifs; enriched by lattice-work and foliated branches, flanking a balustrade and two scrolled branches with leaf form *bobêches* for candles.

Height, 39 inches; width, 16½ inches.

From Sutton-Under-Edge, Gloucestershire, England.

136

561. TWO PAIOT NEEDLEPOINT WALNUT STATE CHAIRS

Louis XIII Period

Rectangular high back, with open voluted and curved arms continuing to supports; approximately square seat, on cabriole legs terminating in *pieds de biches* braced by scrolled X-shape stretcher. Seat and back covered in fine floriated needlework.

(*Illustrated*)

562. TWO PAIOT NEEDLEPOINT WALNUT STATE CHAIRS

Louis XIII Period

Similar to the preceding.

563. TWO PAIOT NEEDLEPOINT WALNUT STATE CHAIRS

Louis XIII Period

Similar to the preceding.

564. TWO PAYOT NEEDLEPOINT WALNUT STATE CHAIRS
Louis XIII Period
Similar to the preceding.

565. TWO PAYOT NEEDLEPOINT WALNUT STATE CHAIRS
Louis XIII Period
Similar to the preceding.

566. CARVED OAK DRESSER   *Jacobean Period*
Rectangular molded top; the front fitted with three paneled draw-
ers having brass knob handles; on vase baluster and block front legs.
Height, 2 feet 6½ inches; length, 5 feet 11 inches.

(*Illustrated*)

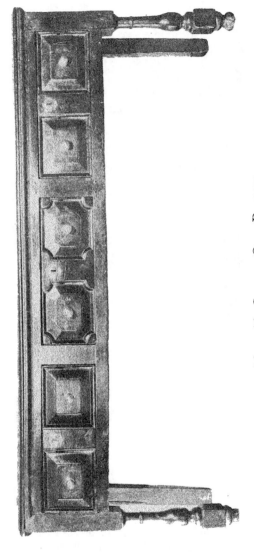

No. 566. Carved Oak Dresser
(*Jacobean Period*)

567. MARQUETERIE WALNUT KNEEHOLE WRITING DESK
Louis XIII Period

Rectangular top in two hinged sections; inlaid with superb floral
marqueterie, which with the frieze opens to fitted interior having
three drawers inlaid with a lozenge motif; the front with eight small
drawers and three larger recessed drawers. On arched bracket
supports.

Height, 31½ inches; length, 36 inches.

140

568. TWO ADAM CARVED PEARWOOD ARMCHAIRS

English, XVIII Century

Oval back; serpentine-shaped seat, which with the arm-rests are covered in fine floriated needlepoint; flaring voluted arms; on reeded tapering legs.

(*Illustrated*)

569. TWO ADAM CARVED PEARWOOD ARMCHAIRS

English, XVIII Century

Similar to the preceding.

570. TWO ADAM CARVED PEARWOOD ARMCHAIRS

English, XVIII Century

Similar to the preceding.

571. Important Carved Mahogany Master's Chair

Chippendale Period

The cartouche-shaped back, serpentined seat, and the arm-rests covered in crimson floral damask. Longitudinally curved and voluted arms projecting beyond incurving supports which join the seat rail slightly back from the front legs. On finely carved cabriole legs with leaf-scroll feet.

Note: This chair is in Chippendale's charmingly restrained French taste.

572. GROS AND PETIT POINT MAHOGANY WING CHAIR

Queen Anne Period

Serpentine crowned back, arched wings and outscrolling arms, supported on short cabriole legs with pad feet. Covered in beautiful needle-point; the back exhibiting the scene of THE NATIVITY, the seat, wings and arms a fine floral design; executed in subdued and charming colors.

573. DECORATIVE OIL PAINTING
                              By Gaspar Verbruggen, Flemish ?—1680

STILL LIFE. Charming arrangement of naturalistic flowers in a jardinière and classic vases resting upon a marble plinth. In the centre of the composition is a curious serpent vase, and flying among the flowers are golden-yellow butterflies. In brilliant colors portrayed with an excellent rendering of values.

Height, 52½ inches; width, 39½ inches.

Signed at lower centre on marble plinth, GASPAR VERBRUGGEN, *and dated 1663.*

574. IMPORTANT WALNUT MARQUETERIE HIGHBOY
                              William and Mary Period

Rectangular, in two sections; cove- and cyma-curved cornice molding, the torus-molded frieze containing a concealed drawer; the front fitted with double enclosing doors, opening to interior fitted with thirteen small drawers and a central cupboard door; the lower section with three graduated drawers on bracket feet. The entire cabinet enriched with superb inlay of arabesque marqueterie and trimmed with original bat's-wing brasses and bail handles.

Height, 5 feet 4 inches; width, 3 feet 4½ inches.

From the Lord Francis Hope Collection and the Collection of Sir Arthur Cory-Wright, Bart., Ayot Place, Welwyn.

(*Illustrated*)

575. CHIPPENDALE CARVED MAHOGANY BREAK-FRONT BOOKCASE
                              English, XVIII Century

Lower part fitted in the centre with two small and three large drawers, flanked on either side by four small drawers; on carved bracket feet; surmounted by one large cabinet and two small cabinets enclosed by glazed panel doors, above which is a shaped cornice carved in a Chinese fretted design.

Length, 6 feet 6 inches; height, 7 feet 9 inches.

144

No. 574. IMPORTANT WALNUT MARQUETERIE HIGHBOY
(*William and Mary Period*)

576. RARE CARVED MAHOGANY TRIPOD TEA-TABLE

Chippendale Period, circa 1770

Tilting top. Very unusual concave octagonal fretted gallery, super-imposed upon the circular top, molded to a series of double cyma-curves with leaf-carved edges; outside the railing are eight dished projections and beneath are the same number of circular trays pivoted to swing out. On superbly carved vase baluster shaft with floriated flutings and tripod support, enriched with leaf and cabochon motifs.

Height, 31 *inches; diameter,* 34 *inches.*

Note: Illustrated by Mr. Herbert Cescinsky in *The Old World House,* Vol. II, page 219.

146

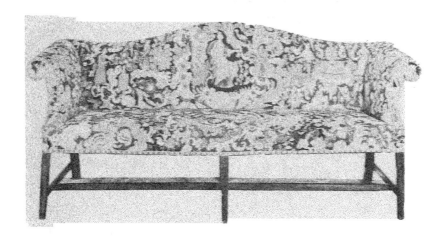

577. Important Gros and Petit Point Mahogany Settee
English, XVIII Century

The serpentined back, outscrolling arms and seat covered with fine needlepoint, depicting on the back central seated figure of a court lady and other figures of an Eastern character. birds, animals and foliage in fine coloring. The seat and arms with birds and foliage. On six tapering square fillet-molded legs braced by an H-stretcher.

Height, 2 feet 11½ inches: length, 6 feet 9¾ inches.

147

IMPORTANT ENGLISH XVIII CENTURY CARVED WALNUT SUITE OF FURNITURE

Beautifully carved in the Style of Charles II during the Georgian period. Each piece covered in contemporary English needlework, exhibiting the coat of arms, crest, insignia and supporters of the first Baron Ranfurly, created 1781, and raised to a Viscounty 1791. The suite has remained in the possession of the Earls of Ranfurly until recently purchased from Northland House, Dungannon, Ireland, the seat of the present Peer, who was Governor General of New Zealand from 1897 to 1904.

DESCRIPTION OF THE RANFURLY ARMS FROM THE OFFICE OF HERALDRY, LONDON

ARMS: Gu. a falcon volant or, within an orle, wavy on the outer, and engrailed on the inner edge, arg. CREST: A falcon close, standing on a perch, ppr. SUPPORTERS: Two falcons, wings inverted ppr: ducally gorged, lined, backed, membered and belled, or. MOTTO: *Moveo et profiteor.*

578. CARVED WALNUT THREE-CHAIR-BACK SETTEE *Georgian Period*
Tall canted back with spiraled uprights, enclosing reticulated, scrolled and voluted leafage, roses and quatrefoils with finely arched cresting, centring the Ranfurly coats of arms; open scrolled and voluted arms; rectangular seat covered in fine needlepoint exhibiting centrally the coat of arms, flanked by the crest; supported by spirally twisted stretchered legs enhanced by fine frontal hooped stretchers. *Height, 54½ inches; length, 64½ inches.*

(*Illustrated*)

578A. CARVED WALNUT THREE-CHAIR-BACK SETTEE *Georgian Period*
Similar to the preceding.

No. 578. Carved Walnut Three-chair-back Settee
(*Georgian Period*)

579. TWO CARVED WALNUT ARMCHAIRS   *Georgian Period*
Similar to and matching the preceding settee, minus the carved coat of arms.

580. SIX CARVED WALNUT SIDE CHAIRS   *Georgian Period*
Similar to and matching the preceding armchairs.

(*One illustrated*)

580A. SIX CARVED WALNUT SIDE CHAIRS   *Georgian Period*
Similar to and matching the preceding armchairs.

581. SIX CARVED WALNUT SIDE CHAIRS   *Georgian Period*
Similar to and matching the preceding side chairs.

(*One illustrated*)

582. TWO CARVED WALNUT STOOLS   *Georgian Period*
Matching the preceding, but having S-scrolled and voluted legs braced by X-shaped stretcher with vase terminal and leaf-carved seat. The needlepoint crested.   *Height, 17½ inches; length, 29½ inches.*

(*One illustrated*)

581   582   580

Nos. 580 and 581. CARVED WALNUT SIDE CHAIRS
(*Georgian Period*)

No. 582. CARVED WALNUT STOOLS
(*Georgian Period*)

151

583. INLAID ROOT WALNUT SLANT-FRONT WRITING-DESK
Queen Anne Period

Rectangular top, with slant-front opening to interior attractively
fitted with six shaped drawers; beneath is a lower drawer and an
ogeed valance; supported on slightly cabriole legs with spade feet.
Banded and cross banded with amboyna wood.

Height, 34½ inches; width, 21½ inches.

584. HEPPLEWHITE CARVED MAHOGANY SECRETARY

English, XVIII Century

In two sections; the recessed superstructure with two-tiered galleried top and having double enclosing doors opening to fitted interior of five harewood drawers and numerous pigeon-holes. The lower section with frieze drawer flanked by carved anthemion motif; fitted with green baize writing top. Supported by four quadrangular fluted legs and block feet. Trimmed with *cuivre doré* handles.

Height, 54 inches; width, 30½ inches.

585. IMPORTANT CHIPPENDALE MAHOGANY SECRETARY-BOOKCASE
English, XVIII Century

In two sections. Rectangular recessed top having swanneck pediment finishing in rosettes, enclosing a lattice design; double enclosing glazed and finely traceried doors. The lower section of serpentine contour; the front fall, which when opened is supported by quadrants, reveals interior fitted with numerous drawers and compartments; the front having four drawers enriched with encarpa motifs and bail handles, the chamfered corners with voluted pilaster blocks. On bracket feet.

Height, 8 feet 3½ inches; width, 3 feet 11 inches.

(*Illustrated*)

586. ADAM CARVED MAHOGANY SECRETARY BOOKCASE
English, XVIII Century

In two sections; the lower, with slant-fall, opening to interior fitted with numerous drawers and compartments; below are two small and three long drawers; on bracket feet. Surmounted by cabinet, enclosed by glazed paneled doors, carved below with urn and festoons in relief.

Length, 37½ inches; height, 7 feet 3 inches.

No. 585. Important Chippendale Mahogany Secretary-bookcase
(*English, XVIII Century*)

587. INLAID SATINWOOD SECRETARY CABINET

English, XVIII Century

Arched recessed superstructure, fitted with five shallow drawers flanked by small cupboards; the doors inlaid with oval medallions of amboyna wood; folding top and frieze drawer. On tapered square legs with spade feet.

Height, 50 inches; width, 29½ inches.

(*Illustrated*)

588. CRIMSON CUT VELVET MAHOGANY WING CHAIR

English, Early XVIII Century

High arched back, slight flaring wings and outscrolling arms; covered in a fine deep crimson cut velvet exhibiting upon an *écru* field bold foliations; supported on molded and collared cabriole legs with pad feet.

589. Kingwood and Tulipwood Writing Table Mounted in
Cuivre Doré

By I. G. Schlichtig, M. E., Louis XV Period

Of curvilinear contour; serpentined top with tooled leather insert;
banded at the edges; the molded underframing fitted with three
drawers finely banded and cross-banded; supported on four slightly
cabriole legs. Richly embellished with superb *cuivre doré* mountings
of the period, finely chiseled and chased.

Height, 2 feet 6 inches; length, 5 feet 5 inches.

Note: Jean Georges Schlichtig, M. E. at Paris, 1765, and later Deputy Councilor
of his corporation. He worked in the Rue St. Nicholas, where he died 1782. His
work is highly esteemed; a commode by his hand bearing the monogram of Marie
Antoinette is in the Louvre.

157.

590. IMPORTANT CARVED WALNUT ARMCHAIR   *Charles II Period*
High canted back, the spiraled uprights enclosing finely carved
and *canné* back surmounted by a cresting centring a coronet
with five roses, the royal emblem.   Carved and voluted arms on
spiral supports; approximately square *canné* seat, on spiraled legs
braced by H-stretcher and a repetition of the cresting as frontal
stretcher.

From the Gwydir Castle Collection.

158

591. IMPORTANT CARVED WALNUT ARMCHAIR

Charles II Period

Canted high back; the spiraled uprights with urn-shaped finials enclose an oval *canné* panel framed and crested by carved scrolled and voluted leafage. Longitudinally curved arms, acanthus-carved and rosetted, projecting beyond spiral supports; *canné* seat on turned and block stretchered legs with bun feet, and an elaborately scrolled frontal stretcher. Loose cushion in Renaissance crimson velvet.

159

592. OIL PAINTING   *By Melchior de Hondecoeter,*
                                         Dutch, 1636-1695

ANIMALISTIC SCENE. Before a charming landscape scene with a well to the right, are naturalistically portrayed male and female species of European fowls in full plumage and of superb coloring. In original frame.

Height, 5 feet 5 inches; length, 7 feet 7 inches.

Signed at the right on a stone of the well with the initials, M. H., *and dated,* 1654.

(*Illustrated*)

593. INLAID KINGWOOD AND TULIPWOOD WRITING TABLE
                                         Louis Seize Period

Rectangular top, with tooled leather insert; the frieze fitted with central drawer having on the left two drawers and on the right one simulating two; a draw slide, with tooled leather insert, at each end; on quadrangular legs; trimmed with *cuivre doré* mounts.

Height, 29 inches; length, 62½ inches.

160

594. INLAID OYSTERED YEW TREE CABINET

William and Mary Period

Rectangular molded top with cyma-molded corners; torus-molded
frieze drawer. double enclosing doors opening to fitted interior of
eleven drawers and central cupboard. The whole finely veneered
in beautifully figured yew exhibiting a geometrical design. On
original stand with frieze drawer; six spiraled legs connected by
incurving stretchers. on bun feet.

Height, 5 feet 5 inches; width. 3 feet 9 inches.

596. CARVED OAK DRESSER   *William and Mary Period*

Rectangular, with superstructure of open shelving; the frieze curiously reticulated in a succession of vase forms; the front fitted
with seven geometrically paneled drawers and a central plainly pan-
cled cupboard door. Trimmed with pierced brasses and bail handles.

Height, 6 feet 5 inches; width, 6 feet 5 inches.

(*Illustrated*)